*Introduction to*
## MUSIC READING
*concepts & applications*

## WADSWORTH MUSIC SERIES

# Introduction to
# MUSIC READING
## concepts & applications

**William Thomson**
*Indiana University*

*Wadsworth Publishing Company, Inc.*
*Belmont, California*

*ACKNOWLEDGEMENTS*

Ch. 5, Melody 37; Ch. 7, Melody 8; Ch. 12, Melody 17; Ch. 13, Melodies 18 and 19; and Ch. 14, Melodies 3 and 8 are reprinted from *Folk Music of Hungary,* by Zoltán Kodály, by permission of the publisher, Barrie & Rockliff.

Ch. 4, Melody 8; Ch. 5, Melodies 28 and 36; Ch. 12, Melodies 14 and 15; and Ch. 14, Melodies 7, 18, and 25 are reprinted from *Hungarian Folk Music,* by Béla Bartók, published by the Oxford University Press, with the permission of Victor Bator, Trustee of the Bartók Estate.

Ch. 14, Melodies 4 and 28 are reprinted by permission of the publisher, J. & W. Chester, Ltd., from *El Retablo de Maese Pedro* and the piano-vocal score of *El Amor Brujo,* by Manuel de Falla.

Ex. 8(a) on p. 237 is reprinted by permission of Aaron Copland, copyright owner, and Boosey and Hawkes, Inc., sole publishers. Copyright 1944 by Aaron Copland.

Ex. 5, p. 221, from *Sight Singing Manual,* Third Edition, by Allen Irvine McHose and Ruth Northup Tibbs. Copyright © 1957 by Appleton-Century-Crofts, Inc.

# PREFACE

The most fundamental requirement for musicianship is the ability to translate the symbols of music notation into the sounds the composer intended—the ability to read music. Evidence is plentiful that experience alone is not an adequate foundation for fluent reading; on the contrary, the reader must learn how to approach any piece of music with understanding before his experience with music can be meaningful.

This book's approach to the problem of building of a foundation for reading begins with the two basic frameworks of musical structure—meter and tonality—and then gradually includes tone patterns that appear in most music of the Western world. The book does not claim to teach complete mastery of techniques for reading all music, but it does establish a good foundation for learning.

*Introduction to Music Reading* is planned for two kinds of students—those who have had no real reading experience, and those who have sung or played an instrument extensively but do not read music with any real assurance. Inexperienced students will find it wise to study the first four chapters thoroughly, until they have a firm grasp of the concepts of meter and tonality. More experienced performers will find that though these first four chapters provide an essential basis for reading music, they can be passed over more rapidly than subsequent chapters. The freshman theory teacher in a college or university "fundamentals" class might regard these first chapters as a review of very basic—and thus quite significant—material.

Beginning with Chapter 4, each chapter is followed by melodies for reading, which exhibit characteristics discussed in the chapter. Sometimes "Practice Melodies" precede "Melodies from Literature" at the end of the chapter; sometimes they are incorporated into the text, indicating that they should be studied and performed before moving on to the next topic. In either case, the "Practice Melodies" incorporate specific problems of reading in a more concentrated form than can be provided by melodies selected from the corpus of folk or composed music.

Although the piano is referred to extensively, particularly in the early discussions of pitch, it should be used sparingly as a guide to pitch recall. When used constantly as a crutch for determining pitch relations, it represents a threat to true musical development. It is not really necessary to use an absolute pitch reference, except when persons with absolute pitch recall would be discomforted. But since it is imperative that all melodies be performed within a range that avoids vocal complications, some source of pitch reference is helpful.

In the beginning (through Chapter 5, perhaps) the reader should refer to numbers derived from scale references or to *sol-fa* syllables as a means of reinforcing his sense of pitch relations to tonic. Since both of these symbolic systems are crutches, however, and not germane to the reading of music, they should be discarded as soon as the reader has developed the ability to recall the pitch relations within any given pitch system. Thereafter, only neutral syllables (such as "la") are recommended, except where reading difficulties might be surmounted most easily by reference to the symbolic names.

Five chapters—6, 9, 10, 11, and 12—deal with two different topics, since neither topic really demands separate treatment. The teacher may prefer, of course, to assign each topic as a separate unit, selecting appropriate melodies at the ends of the chapters.

William Thomson

# CONTENTS

# 1

## TIME AND NOTATION IN MUSIC

### ORGANIZATION OF TIME INTO METER

The sounds of music are organized in time by the grouping process we call *meter*. It is simpler to think of any series of things in time—whether they be the ticks of a clock or the events of a life—as grouped elements rather than separate, unorganized units. In music, time is divided by equally spaced pulses (or *beats*), which are grouped by twos or threes. The meter of a march (which must coincide with the strides of two marching feet) usually is organized in groups of two. The meter of a waltz, on the other hand, is a grouping in threes, because this dance is basically a movement of the feet in a one-two-three pattern.

A series of equally spaced pulses can represent a meter only if some of the pulses are differentiated from the others in a regular pattern. If we clap pattern (a) below, nothing suggests a march, but if we make every other clap louder (with the accent sign >), it is easy to imagine the "LEFT–right, LEFT–right" impulse of a march. (We shall let the sign X represent a clap in the next few illustrations of divided time.)

Example 1

(a)

X  X  X  X  X  X  X  X  X  X  X  X ‖

(b)

$\overset{>}{X}$  X  $\overset{>}{X}$  X  $\overset{>}{X}$  X  $\overset{>}{X}$  X  $\overset{>}{X}$  X  $\overset{>}{X}$  X ‖

We can suggest the motion of a waltz by accenting our claps to form groups of three:

Example 2

(c)

$\overset{>}{X}$  X  X  $\overset{>}{X}$  X  X  $\overset{>}{X}$  X  X  $\overset{>}{X}$  X  X ‖

We can achieve the same sort of organization of time if we clap some of the continuing pulses of a series and merely *imagine* the remaining claps in each group. For example:

Example 3

(d)

X  .  X  .  X  .  X  .  X  .  X  . ‖

This is still a duple (or two-part) grouping, just as (e) is still definitely a triple (or three-part) grouping.

Example 4

(e)

X  X  .  X  X  .  X  X  .  X  X  . ‖

In patterns (b) and (c) a meter, or *measuring*, was created psychologically because some claps, being stronger, acted as focal points of the group. In (d) and (e), some of the claps can, in effect, be said to "last longer," since each unclapped pulse blends in to form an imagined prolongation of the clapped pulse that precedes it. An accent resulting from a stronger sound, as in (b) and (c), is called a *dynamic accent*; an accent produced because one sound of a series has a relatively greater duration, as in (d) and (e), is called an *agogic accent*. We shall return to both of these means for creating a feeling of meter in subsequent chapters.

## TIME IN MUSICAL NOTATION

   The claps used in the first section to illustrate accent and meter are just one way of marking the passage of time by sounds. The *X* used to represent a clap sometimes serves a similar purpose in drum parts in a musical score. But these pulses usually are represented in musical notation by signs such as the *quarter note* (♩), the *eighth note* (♪), and the *half note* (𝅗𝅥). If we rewrite pattern (a) as below, with a quarter note replacing each *X* to represent the span of time from one pulse to the next, it is read to sound exactly as before.

Example 5

In this case, the quarter note represents the periodic division of time; we can say that the *basic duration* of this series is the quarter note.

   When a note is sung or played, however, it must last longer than the sound of a clap, which has only a momentary duration. We can define the basic duration more precisely by saying that it represents a sound that lasts from the beginning of one pulse until the beginning of the next.

Example 6

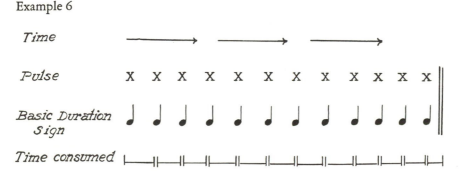

   To write a march rhythm with the quarter note as the basic duration, we would use measures of two quarter notes each, or $\frac{2}{4}$ meter. Vertical lines, or *bars,* replace the accent signs used in the earlier metered examples to mark the groups dividing the whole series into measures.

Example 7

(f)

This pattern is the same, of course, as pattern (b). If we chose the half note (♩) or the eighth note (♪) to represent the basic duration, the pattern would still be the same. Each of the following patterns represents the same sound relationships as (b), (d), and (f).

Example 8

(g)

(h)

A waltz rhythm in which the quarter note is the basic duration would be notated in measures of three quarter notes each, or $\frac{3}{4}$ meter. Again, vertical bars mark off the whole series into groups or measures.

Example 9

The same result could be achieved by replacing the quarter note as the basic duration with the half note or eighth note, as shown for the duple meters. This interchangeability of basic durations can be bothersome for the beginning reader, for he must learn to read music in which different note values represent the basic division of time.

## DIVISIONS AND MULTIPLES OF THE BASIC DURATION

Music would be very dull indeed if it consisted only of tones whose durations were equal to the basic duration. Rhythms usually consist of tones that are divisions or multiples of the basic duration of a meter, in addition to the basic duration itself. In meters whose basic duration is the quarter note, the simplest multiple is a half note (♩+♩=♩), and the simplest division is two eighth notes (♪♪ or ♫).[1] Thus two eighth notes are equal in duration to one quarter note, and one half note equals two quarter notes. Meters with two-part divisions of the basic duration are known as *simple meters.* We shall discuss *compound meters,* which use a three-part division, in Chapter 8.

Sing "la" on any comfortable pitch for the following patterns. Clap the pulse as you sing the proper note durations.

---

[1] The separate notes are *flagged*; the connected notes are *beamed*. For our present purposes we may regard flagged and beamed notes of the same duration as interchangeable.

Example 10

Keep the same duration for the quarter note while singing the next pattern, still using claps or some motion of the body (tap on a desk, for example) to represent the continuing pulse. Make certain that any pair of eighth notes (as in measures two and three) fills the same duration as the neighboring quarter notes.

Example 11

Maintaining the same duration for the quarter note, sing the next pattern, in which *multiples* of the basic duration occur. Make certain here that each half note lasts as long as *two* basic durations.

Example 12

As mentioned earlier, the same principle of multiplying and dividing notes can be applied to meters in which other note values represent the basic duration. The simplest multiples and divisions for the basic durations of three common meters are shown below.

| BASIC DURATION | SIMPLEST MULTIPLE | SIMPLEST DIVISION |
| --- | --- | --- |
| quarter | half | eighths |
| half | whole | quarters |
| eighth | quarter | sixteenths |

Establish a steady but comfortable pulse rate for the basic duration and sing each of the following patterns on a single pitch (intoning "la"). If you wish, use a pitch pipe or piano for a specific pitch. Clap or tap the pulse for each pattern.

PRACTICE PATTERNS

(a) *basic duration =* ♩

(b) *basic duration =* ♩

(c) *basic duration =* ♩

(d) *basic duration =* ♩

(e) *basic duration =* ♩

(f) *basic duration =* ♪

(g) *basic duration =* ♩

(h) *basic duration =* ♩

(i) *basic duration =* ♪

(j) *basic duration =* ♩

$\frac{3}{4}$ ♩♩♩ | ♩ ♩ | ♫♩♩ | ♩ ♩ | ♩♩♩♫ | ♩♩♩ | ♩ ♩ ‖

(k) *basic duration =* ♩

₵² ♩ ♩ | ○ | ♩ ♩ ♩ | ♩ ♩ ♩ | ♩ ♩ | ○ | ♩ ♩ ♩ | ○ ‖

Each of the patterns above is comparatively dull because it consists of incessant sound. Most music is not so totally occupied by tone, for many rhythms consist of the interplay of sound and silence. Specific signs are used in music notation to represent the durations of silences.

**RESTS**

*quarter rest* 𝄽 (*silence for duration of* ♩ )
*eighth rest* 𝄾 (*silence for duration of* ♪ )
*half rest* ▬ (*silence for duration of* ♩ )
*whole rest* ▬ (*silence for duration of* ○ )
*sixteenth rest* 𝄿 (*silence for duration of* ♬ )

It is customary to use the whole rest to signify any measure of total silence, no matter what the basic duration of the meter may be. (Since it would be difficult to make any sound for a measure in which no notes appear, it is really immaterial what sign is used.) Notice that the whole rest differs from the half rest only in that it is drawn below a line of the staff (almost always the fourth line from the bottom) rather than above.

Example 13

*whole rest*          *half rest*

Clap a steady pulse for each of the next patterns, singing the notes as they are indicated. (Sing "la.") When a rest appears, continue with your clapping to keep a steady pulse while your voice is silent.

*PRACTICE PATTERNS*

(a) $\frac{2}{4}$ ♩ ♩ | 𝄽 ♩ | ♩ ♩ | 𝄽 ♩ | ♩ ♩ | ♩ | ♩ ♩ | ♩ ‖
       x x | x x | *etc.*

---

² This meter sign indicates "cut time" or, more accurately, *alla breve*. It is the same as $\frac{2}{2}$ meter.

(b) 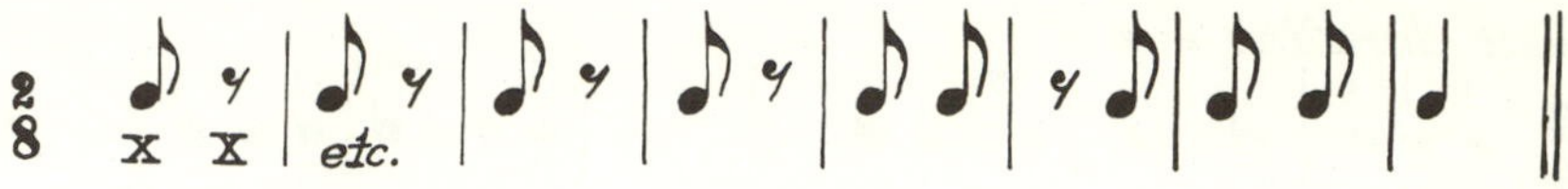


(c) 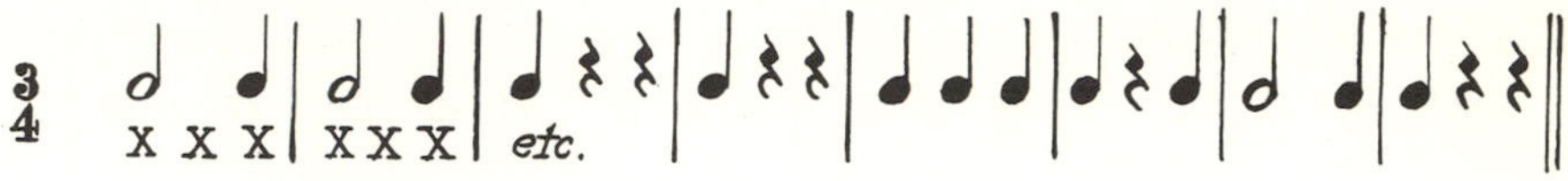


(d) 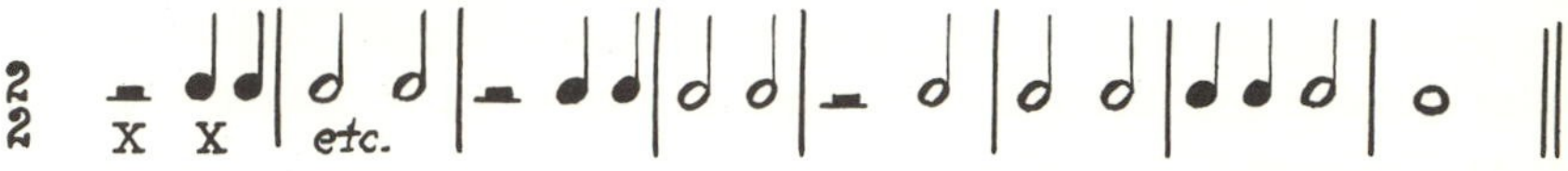


(e) 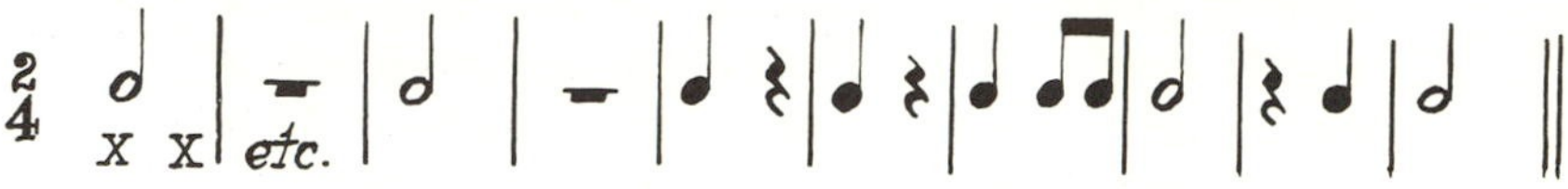


(f) 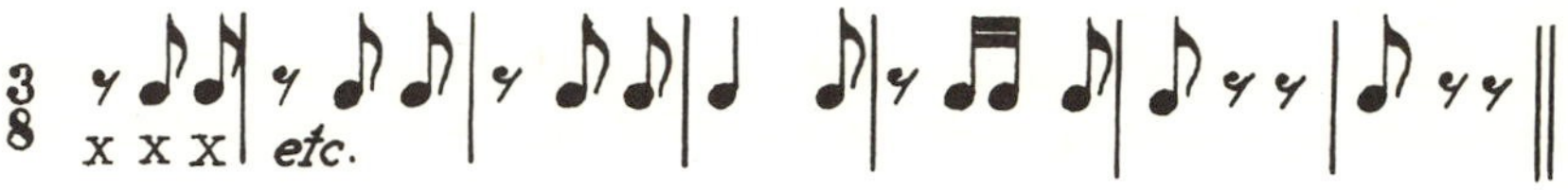


(g) 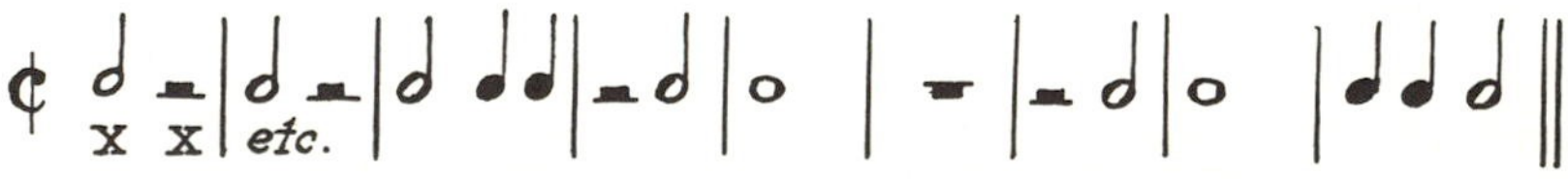


(h) 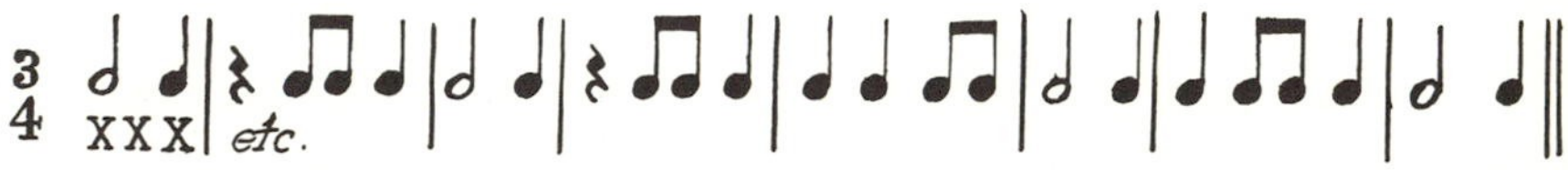


(i) 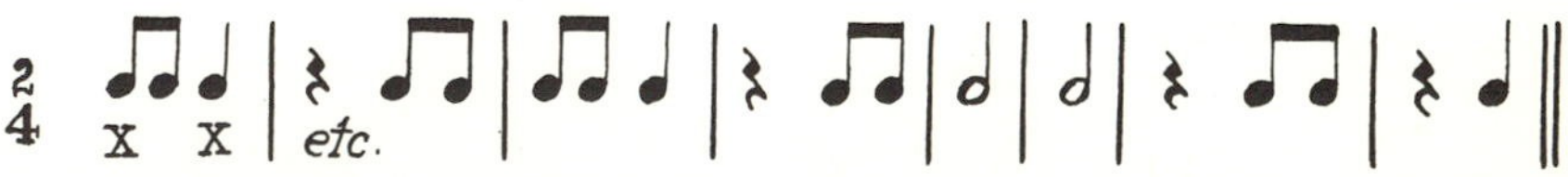


(j) 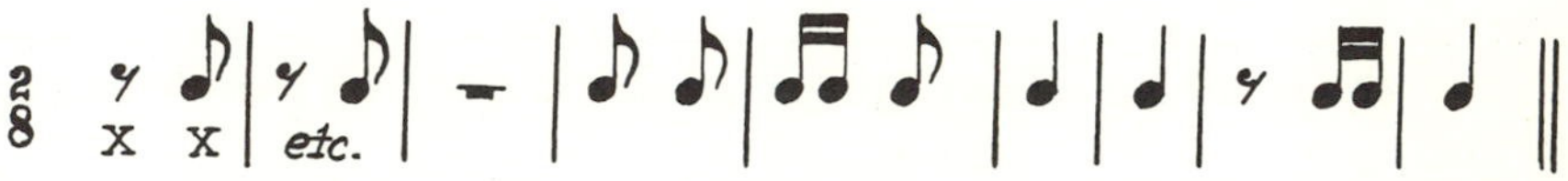

A dot increases the duration of any note by one-half. For example, a dotted half note is equal in duration to a half note plus a quarter note. ( 𝅗𝅥. = 𝅗𝅥 + ♩ ). In a meter with a basic duration of a quarter note, then, a dotted half note would last through three basic durations:

Similarly, a dotted quarter has a duration equal to a quarter plus an eighth note ( ♩. = ♩ + ♪ ), and a dotted eighth is equal in duration to an eighth plus a sixteenth note ( ♪. = ♪ + 𝅘𝅥𝅯 ).

Increased duration can also be indicated by a *tie* sign ( ⌢ or ⌣ ) connecting two note heads. This sign merely indicates that the second note is not articulated separately; thus the two values are joined into a continuous tone. For example, the combination ♩‿♩ has the same duration as a half note, and the combination 𝅗𝅥‿♩ has the same duration as a dotted half. The tie sign is frequently used to join two notes across a bar line.

Clap or tap the pulse while you sing the following patterns, which contain tied and/or dotted notes.

## PRACTICE PATTERNS

(a) sing clap  2/4 ...

(b) 3/4 ...

(c) 2/2 ...

(d) 2/4 ...

(e) 3/8 ...

(f) [musical notation in 2/4 time]

(g) [musical notation in 3/4 time]

(h) [musical notation in 2/8 time]

(i) [musical notation in cut time]

(j) [musical notation in 3/2 time]

## BASIC CONDUCTING PATTERNS

Another way of representing the "count," or onward flow of time, in music is by moving the hand and arm in a conducting pattern. This is the basic method used by a conductor to convey to performers the steady progression of pulses in the music they are performing. Each meter—two-beat, three-beat, or four-beat—is represented by a slightly different hand-arm motion.

For any two-beat, or duple, meter, such as $\frac{2}{4}$, $\frac{2}{2}$, or $\frac{2}{8}$, a two-part pattern is used, usually with the right hand and arm moving together. (The left-handed conductor will reverse the motion.)

Example 14

Example 15 illustrates this motion in conjunction with a line of notes.

Example 15

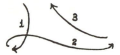

The pattern for any triple meter of medium tempo, such as the previous examples in $\frac{3}{4}$, $\frac{3}{2}$, and $\frac{3}{8}$, is a three-part motion.

Example 16

In conjunction with a note pattern the hand would move as follows:

Example 17

Quadruple meters are divisible, of course, into duple units. For this reason a two-beat conducting pattern would suffice as a guide to the performance of any four-pulse meter such as $\frac{4}{8}$ or $\frac{4}{4}$.[3] A four-beat pattern (Example 18) has the advantage, however, of indicating to the performer the four-pulse organization of each measure. The first pulse is strongest; the next three are weak-strong-weak.

Example 18

In conjunction with a quadruple-meter phrase, the hand motion would be as follows (note that motions for the first and third beats cover more space and must therefore be more rapid):

Example 19

---

[3] In modern notation, the meter signature $\mathbf{C}$ is the same as $\frac{4}{4}$.

Practice each of these conducting patterns while counting out two, three, or four pulses per measure, at first aloud, later silently. Do this until you can keep each pattern going without paying undivided attention to it. Then sing the following rhythms while keeping the pulse with the appropriate conducting pattern. Use the syllable "la."

*PRACTICE PATTERNS*

(k) $\frac{2}{4}$ [musical notation]

(l) ¢ [musical notation]

(m) $\frac{3}{2}$ [musical notation]

(n) $\frac{4}{4}$ [musical notation]

As soon as you can perform each of the preceding patterns with some fluency, write similar patterns of your own, using only the notes, rests, and meters presented in this chapter. Perform these for fellow students, who should notate them from your performance.

# 2

## PITCH IN MUSIC

### PITCH NOTATION

From a musical point of view, the patterns we dealt with in Chapter 1 are not very interesting, for they lack the variety of sounds that creates what we call *melody*. Although rhythm alone—the rhythms of a drum, for example —can be uniquely engaging, differences of pitch—highness and lowness of sounds—provide the additional facet of tone

Example 1  Natural notes of the great staff and the piano keyboard

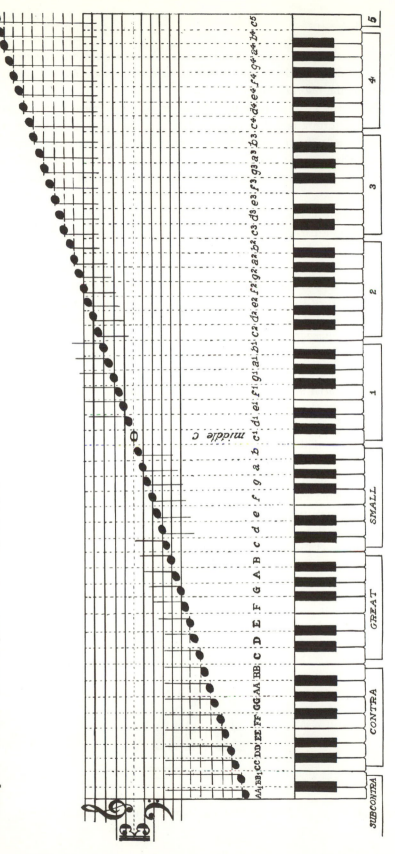

that we consider necessary in music. Just as time in music is represented by the various note symbols of musical notation, the precise pitches of these note values can be represented by their placement on the *musical staff.*

The staff is a visual frame that shows the exact placement of the sounds you must produce to perform a melody accurately. The *great staff* provides a line or a space position for every pitch of our musical system; Example 1 shows every note on the great staff that corresponds to a white key on the piano keyboard. We shall deal with only a small portion of the available pitches, for the singing voice cannot produce such a wide range.

In Example 1, you will see that the letter name for each of the keys is written in a way that denotes a particular pitch level; the keys in the middle portion of the keyboard are named $c^1$, $d^1$, $e^1$, $f^1$, $g^1$, $a^1$, $b^1$, while those to the right repeat the same letter names with superscripts of $^2$ rather than $^1$. This system of signs is used to describe *registration,* the location of a particular pitch. Notice further that no superscripts accompany the letter names to the left of the $c^1$ portion of the keyboard. This pitch register is called the *small octave* (or *small eight notes*), since a lower case ("small") letter is the identifying mark. The octave to the left of the small octave, whose notes are identified by capital letters, is called the *great octave.* Still lower is the *contraoctave,* and the three remaining notes on the keyboard are in the *subcontraoctave.* We shall use these precise note names only when they are crucial in speaking about a particular pitch or pitch relationship; otherwise we shall use capital letters to identify all pitches.

The signs that appear at the left of a musical staff are called *clefs.* The two shown within the lines of the great staff in Ex. 1 are the *treble,* or *G, clef* (𝄞), and the *bass,* or *F, clef* (𝄢). Between these is the *movable,* or *C, clef* (𝄡), which is found in various places on the musical staff but always denotes the pitch of middle C. We shall deal with only the treble and bass clefs at present; work with the C clef must await considerable experience with the other two.

The treble clef, which curls around the second line of the staff to locate the note $g^1$, is normally used for higher-pitched instruments, such as female voices and clarinets. You will remember that this note is to the right of the piano's middle C, or $c^1$.

Example 2

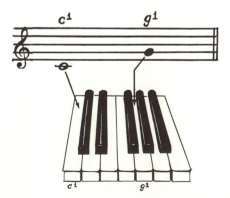

If the second staff line is $g^1$, the remaining note names of the staff are as follows:

Example 3

Note that the number of notes represented on the staff can be increased by the use of segmental lines, called *ledger* (or *leger*) *lines,* which are drawn parallel to the staff lines as with *c¹* and *a²* above.

The bass clef locates the pitch *f* on the staff as the second line from the top. This is *f* below middle *C* on the piano.

Example 4

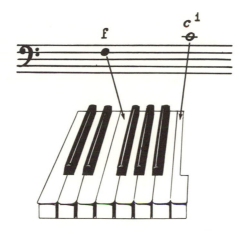

If we fill the remaining lines and spaces of the bass staff, the note names will be as follows:

Example 5

Using both the treble and bass clefs yields a set of twenty-five different pitches from one ledger line below to one ledger line above.

Example 6

If we played all of these notes at the piano we would strike only the white keys, thus omitting seventeen other pitches in this span, which are of equal importance in music. (To retrace the evolution of musical notation and the development of the piano keyboard's division into black and white keys would go beyond the scope of this book.) We can regard the white-key notes of the piano, the *natural* notes depicted by unaltered signs on the staff, as a basic set of pitches to which other pitches can be added. The names of these additional notes are derived from those of the natural notes—for example, "*A*-flat" and "*F*-sharp."

## THE CHROMATIC PITCH SERIES

The natural set of notes from $c^1$ to $c^2$ contains seven different pitches.

Example 7

But the music of western civilization uses a number of other pitches within this gamut. An examination of the piano keyboard will show that the black keys make five pitches available in addition to the seven shown above. These fill in the eight-note (or *octave*) range as illustrated.

Example 8

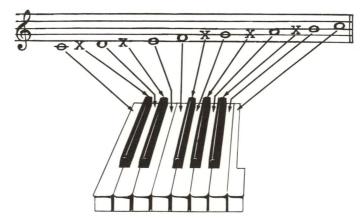

These additional notes, called *chromatics* (*chroma* = color), are named and notated in a simple way that distinguishes them from the natural notes of the staff and the white keys of the piano. By adding an *accidental*—a *sharp* (♯) or *flat* (♭)—to the left (in musical notation) or to the right (in ordinary writing) of any natural note, a new pitch is represented. A sharp raises the pitch of a natural note by one half step; a flat lowers the pitch by one half step. We shall refer to the piano keyboard again for a clear representation.

Example 9

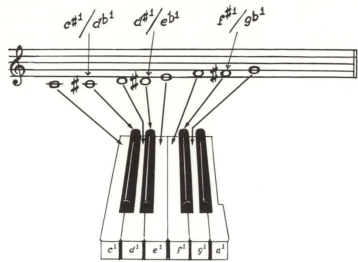

Between any *C* and the next *D* on the keyboard there is a black key, which produces a pitch that lies midway between the two. This pitch might be called *C*♯ or *D*♭, for it is one half step higher than *C* and one half step lower than *D*. Similarly, the black key between *F* and *G* makes a sound that can be called *F*♯ or *G*♭.

Example 10

The additional five pitches within any octave make a total of twelve pitches that are basic to music of the Western world.

Example 11

### PITCH ORGANIZATION IN MELODY: THE TONALITY FRAME

So far we have discussed only the notation and nomenclature of musical pitch. The really fundamental problem in music reading is to learn how pitches are strung together to produce *melody*.

Just as we discussed meter as a *time frame* for tonal organization, we shall regard tonality as a *pitch frame*. Tonality is a property of a melody in which one pitch, the *tonic*, serves as a kind of focal point, an ultimate reference for all other pitches within the melody.

Sing through one verse of "America" and notice that the last tone represents the most satisfactory resolution of the entire series of pitches; no other pitch can serve this function quite so well.

Example 12     America

Notice also that this last pitch is the same as the first (here written as $c^1$) and that this same pitch occurs more times in this melody than almost any other pitch. For these reasons alone we might conclude that $C$ is the tonic pitch of this melody; it dominates the melodic pattern.

A close look at this melody will reveal still another significant factor that helps to make $C$ tonic rather than another pitch; the whole melody is outlined by the framework of $c^1$-$g^1$. We shall call this framework the *tonality frame*. (Tonality frame and pitch range are not always the same. Note that in "America" one note lies a step above the tonality frame of $c^1$-$g^1$.) We can see other tonality frames organizing other familiar melodies in essentially the same way.

Example 13

(a)     Joy to the World

Joy to the world! the Lord is come. Let earth re-
ceive her King. Let ev - ry - heart pre-pare Him

(b) London Bridge[1]

(c) Lullaby (Brahms)

The tonality frames of the melodies above encompass two tonal distances: the frames of melodies (a) and (c) span an octave, while melody (b), like "America," has a frame that spans five notes, or a *fifth*. The tonality frames of (a) and (c) extend from tonic to tonic, while those of "America" and "London Bridge" extend from tonic to *dominant*. The latter term denotes the pitch that stands a fifth above any tonic pitch.

The *generic* sizes of intervals in music notation are measured by counting the lines and spaces from one of the notes up or down to the other.

---

[1]Observe that the flagging of notes in these two songs corresponds to the division of words in the texts. In vocal music it is customary to *beam* successive notes only when they carry the same syllable of the text.

Example 14

The dominant relation of any tonic note lies a fifth higher or a fourth lower. Either direction yields the same note.

Example 15

We shall discuss additional kinds of tonality frames in subsequent sections of our study, but for the present our attention will center upon the tonic-dominant relation, because it is the tonality frame in many melodies, as well as an easy pitch relation to sing and to remember.

Each of the following melodies is composed of only two pitches, *tonic* and *dominant*. Note that each melody duplicates the rhythms presented in Chapter 1 on page 9. If you have any difficulty in reading one of the melodies below, refer to the corresponding example (which uses only one pitch) for practice, before proceeding. For pitch orientation, play and sing the tonality frame, which consists here of the only pitches in the melody, before practicing each of these simple melodies. Always clap, tap, or conduct one full measure before singing. Use these melodies for dictation with other students, having them notate from your performance.

## PRACTICE PATTERNS

Sing with "la":

(c)

(d)

(e)

(f)

(g)

(h)

(i)

(j)

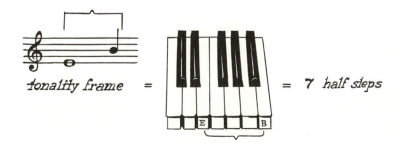

Every tonic or dominant in the preceding melodies is a natural note. This is not true, of course, for all tonic-dominant relationships; sometimes flat or sharp notes are used.

The tonality frames of all the preceding melodies contain the same number of half steps. This can be seen most clearly by looking at a piano keyboard.

Example 16

melody (a)

melody (b)

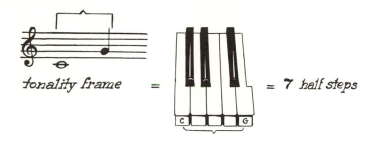

melody (c)

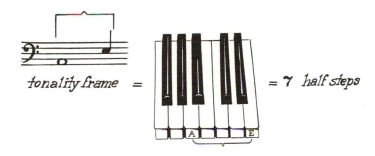

This particular fifth—the *perfect fifth*—consists of seven half steps or *semitones;* the same interval can also be described as 3½ tones, since there are two semitones in every whole tone.

A fifth (determined by counting inclusive lines and spaces of the staff) that is smaller or larger than 3½ tones is not a perfect fifth. For example, the fifth below, *B* to *F*, is only three tones (six semitones) wide.

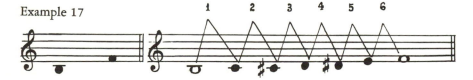

We could do one of two things to make this interval a perfect fifth: lower the *B* to *B♭*, or raise the *F* to *F♯*.

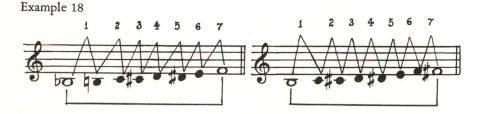

The interval *B-F*, which is one semitone smaller than a perfect fifth, is called a *diminished fifth*. If it had been a semitone larger than a perfect fifth, it would have been an *augmented fifth*.

This peculiarity of interval names is a result of our musical staff and its fixed pitch representation, which consists of an *unequal* set of relations. Although all of the lines are the same distance apart, the pitches they represent are not. The line-spaces *E-F* and *B-C* represent semitone distances, while all other line-space or space-line successions represent whole tone distances.

Example 19

The ability to name interval sizes can be learned only through practice. One principle to remember is that any fifth above a natural note is a *perfect* fifth if it also is a natural note, with the sole exception of *B-F*. (This is true, of course, no matter what clef is used.)

Example 20

Any alteration by flat or sharp of one of the natural notes in a perfect fifth necessitates a corresponding alteration of the other note *if a perfect fifth is required*.

Example 21

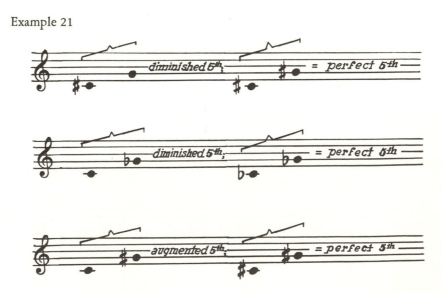

Inverting a fifth produces a fourth.

Example 22

A *perfect* fourth is one whole tone smaller than a perfect fifth, spanning a pitch distance of five semitones (2½ whole tones). As with the perfect fifth, any fourth above a natural note is a *perfect fourth* except *F-B*.

Example 23

And again like the fifth, any fourth that is a semitone smaller than a perfect fourth (spanning only four semitones) is a *diminished* fourth, while any fourth that is a semitone larger than a perfect fourth is an *augmented* fourth.

Example 24

The practice patterns in this chapter include only perfect fifths and fourths. For future reference, however, one should learn to identify all interval sizes by sound, sight, and name. Identify each of the intervals below. To learn to recognize intervals with ease, return to this page frequently and read the interval names off at a fixed rate.

## INTERVAL IDENTIFICATION

All of the melodies in the following practice section have tonality frames of tonic up to dominant, or perfect fifths. Follow the procedure used for the melodies on page 22 in practicing these new examples. Tap or clap the basic duration for initial readings; use the appropriate conducting pattern for later readings. Note that an accidental affects a note every time it appears after the accidental in that measure. For example, measure (a) must be performed as shown in (b), but (c) must be performed as in (d).

Example 25

(c)                       (d)

## PRACTICE PATTERNS

(a)

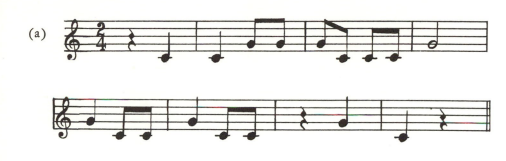

(b)

(c)

(d)

(e)

(f)

All of the preceding practice patterns have consisted of a tonic and its dominant above. The simplest variant of this basic pitch framework occurs in melodies where the dominant is below its tonic rather than above, producing a tonality frame of a perfect fourth rather than a perfect fifth. The next four melodies are based on this perfect-fourth relationship—tonic above, dominant below. Always play the pitches of the tonality frame before attempting to sing the whole pattern. Notice that the tonic note has been shown in the tonality frame as a longer duration than the dominant, because of its greater structural significance.

*PRACTICE PATTERNS*

(i) Tonality frame

As soon as you can perform the melodies here and on the previous pages with fluency, make up melodies of your own that use the note values already introduced and have tonality frames of tonic-dominant or dominant-tonic. Use these for dictation practice in class or with another student.

# 3

## BROADENING
## THE PITCH RANGE

*THE OCTAVE AS TONALITY FRAME*

Two of the melodies in Ex. 13, Chapter 2, had tonality frames of an octave. Though this is a more common span for a melody than the fifth and fourth, it is not always easy to sing pitches this far apart with accuracy without learning patterns of a more restricted range first. Both "Joy to the World" and Brahms' "Lullaby" are organized within a tonic-to-tonic outline. Each of the practice patterns below has the same kind of tonality frame, with the dominant between the tonic notes. As before, play or sing the pitches of each tonality frame before singing the melody.

*PRACTICE MELODIES*

Another way in which the octave can act as the pitch outline for a melody is found in melodies which extend from dominant to dominant, with the tonic pitch in between. Though the interval between these outer notes of the tonality frame is still an octave, it has a slightly different effect, for now it is 5-5 rather than the more familiar 1-1 (or tonic-tonic). Notice that this kind of tonality frame is actually a combination of two patterns learned earlier: the tonic-dominant, which was the basis for the patterns on page 29, and the dominant-tonic, which outlined the melodies on pages 30–32.

Example 1[1]

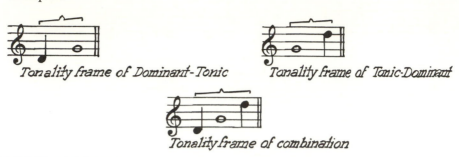

*Tonality frame of Dominant-Tonic*          *Tonality frame of Tonic-Dominant*

*Tonality frame of combination*

### PRACTICE MELODIES

---

[1] The greater importance of tonic is symbolized in all analyses by a note of greater duration.

The same kinds of tonality frames—dominant-dominant octave and tonic-tonic octave—constitute the structural outlines of many familiar melodies. Now that we have become acquainted with these pitch bases, we can begin to draw closer to patterns which are more interesting as melodies, by adding other pitches to this rudimentary melodic "vocabulary."

## THE MEDIANT PITCH

There is another pitch that is easy to remember and sing, about midway between the tonic and dominant. Its name, *mediant,* reflects its position.

Example 2

Note that this new pitch cuts the tonic-dominant fifth into two thirds:

Example 3

These thirds are not of the same size; in this example, $c^1$ and $e^1$ are two whole tones (or four semitones) apart, while $e^1$ and $g^1$ are only $1\frac{1}{2}$ whole tones apart. The larger of these intervals is known as a *major* ("big") *third;* the smaller is known as a *minor* ("little") *third.* These two sizes of thirds play a significant role in music, for the presence of one or the other helps to determine a melody's *modality.* A melody that consistently uses the major third above tonic is said to have a *major modality;* a melody that consistently uses the minor third above tonic is said to have a *minor modality.*[2] Notice that in the tonic-dominant relation a minor third inserted above tonic produces a major third between the mediant and dominant.

Example 4

Adding the mediant, or third, above tonic makes possible melodic patterns of greater musical interest. Before practicing each of the patterns below, determine its tonality frame and notate it in the space provided, as in (a). Play the tonic pitch on a piano

---

[2] Modality will be discussed further in later chapters, particularly Chapters 5 and 12.

or pitch pipe, then sing the pitches of the tonality frame. Establish a steady pulse that is not too fast (tapping, clapping, or beating the appropriate conductor's pattern), and sing the melody. Note the introduction of *slurs* ( ⌣ ) in the melodies to indicate logical groupings. For the present these marks can be regarded as indications for breathing; each section enclosed within a slur is to be performed in a single breath.

*PRACTICE MELODIES*

## SIMPLE CHORD NOMENCLATURE

All of the preceding melodies used the *tonic*, *dominant*, and *mediant* pitches exclusively. These tones combine in a melody to form a simple structural pattern called the *tonic triad* or *tonic chord*. Many musicians reserve the term "chord" for pitches sounded simultaneously, but it is quite acceptable to borrow the same term to describe the cohesive effect that pitches produce when they are sounded successively, as in a melody. The preceding melodies were simple largely because they used the pitches of just one chord, the tonic.

Simple chords, such as those we have been using as the basis of our reading patterns, are classified according to the kinds of intervals that compose them. For example, the chord basis of melody (1) on page 41 is major, because its mediant forms a major third with its tonic.

Example 5

On the other hand, the chord basis of melody (k) is minor, for its mediant forms a minor third above its tonic.

Example 6

The notes that constitute a simple chord are given names associated with their relative positions. The tonic in any major or minor triad is called the *root,* for it is the most important member. The remaining members are named in accordance with their interval relations to the root pitch. In Ex. 6, *F* is the third and *A* is the fifth.

A major or minor triad can be scrambled so that it looks quite different, but its basic structure will still determine its classification as a chord. For example, chord (a) and its three rearrangements, (b), (c), and (d), are all known as "*C*-major triads," and all have *G* as their fifth and *E* as their third.

Example 7

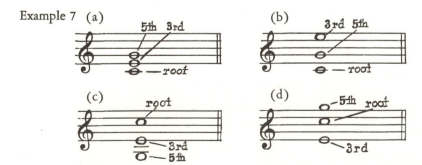

It should be clear, then, that the classification of a chord is derived from its simplest form. In this form, the notes lie within a single octave, the fifth is actually an interval of a fifth above the root, and the third lies between the root and the fifth—as in (a) above. Another way of describing this simplest form, or *root position,* in terms of notation on the staff, would be to say that the three notes are placed on three successive lines or three successive spaces. We can readily see that neither of the chords below is in its simplest form, because (a) uses a space and two lines, while the notes of (b) lie on two spaces and one line.

Example 8

To put the same notes *(D, G, B)* in their simplest form, or *root position,* we must arrange them on successive lines of the staff, as in Ex. 9(c), or an octave lower, as in (d), where successive spaces are employed.

Example 9

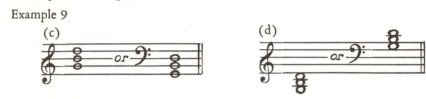

Renotate the following chords so that they appear in their root positions. Then name the chord type (major or minor). Some appear in their simplest forms already; when this is the case, leave the space blank.

The exercise below is to be performed at a piano or with a pitch pipe. For each written note, you are to sing the required chord in the following way: (1) play the given pitch, (2) sing the given pitch, (3) sing the chord's fifth, (4) sing the chord's third, and (5) sing the chord's root again. You can use the number "one" as a syllable for the root, thus establishing a "text" of "one, five, three, one"—or use the syllables *do, sol, mi, do."*

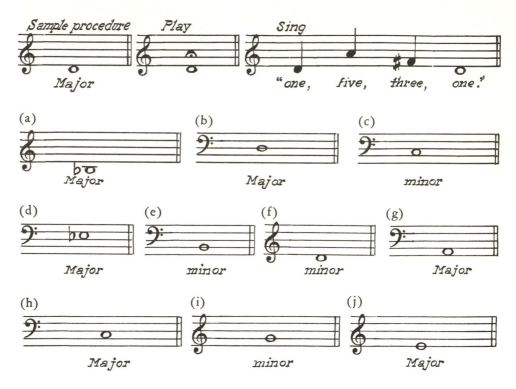

Now repeat the exercises, visualizing the actual notes "five" and "three" as they lie on the staff, and singing their letter names. This is not easy at first, so proceed slowly, making certain that your triadic spellings are always accurate. Check at the piano if necessary, but don't rely too much on this means of correction.

To carry this kind of practice further, sit at the keyboard and play any pitch at random, to serve as the root of a major or minor triad. Then sing this pitch as "one," followed by the "five," "three," "one" of the complete chord. Or let the chosen pitch represent "five" or "three" rather than "one," and sing the remaining members of the major or minor triad.

# 4

## *MELODIC STRUCTURE*

When mentally projected upon the notes of any passage, the tonality frame serves as a guide to which any pitch can be related. We will now begin to add other pitch relationships to the basic framework of *tonic, dominant,* and *mediant* notes which we have developed in the three previous chapters.

### BASIC PITCHES IN MELODY

Most melodies are organized so that some pitches are more important structurally than others. This can happen for one or all of the following reasons:

1. Greater duration (agogic accent) or repetition.
2. Metric accent (first note in measure or third pulse of a four-pulse meter).
3. Contextual location: first pitch or last pitch in a melody, highest or lowest pitch of a pattern, or final pitch of a melodic segment.
4. Role as a member of the tonality frame.

Each of these four points can be seen in the simple folksong below.

Example 1    Denmark

Note that the circled notes provide a basic scaffolding for the total structure. In this melody, all these basic pitches happen to be tonic, dominant, or mediant. This is by no means always the case, but for the present we shall limit our examples to these simpler melodies.

We could make a melodic abstraction of the melody above by showing on a staff only those notes that, because of their prominence in the melody, can be regarded as basic. In this abstract representation, we shall indicate structural importance in the melody by note values: basic pitches are white notes, decorative pitches are black—here shown in parentheses to further emphasize their purely decorative role.

Example 2

The basic pitches of this melody, *D*, *A*, and *F*♯, serve as a background that makes it easy to determine the exact locations of the remaining notes, *E* and *G*: *E* is between *tonic* and *mediant,* while *G* lies between *mediant* and *dominant.*

The following melody is similar to that of Ex. 1.

Example 3    U.S.

Here the tonic (*G*), the dominant (*D*), and the mediant (*B*) serve as the basic pitches, since they occur in accented metric positions and have relatively greater durations than the only remaining pitch, *A*.

As measures three to five demonstrate, a melody may hover around a single basic pitch for longer than one measure. As a rule of thumb when dealing with simple melodies, however, the measure may be regarded as the "usual sphere of pitch organization," thus yielding one basic pitch per measure.

## DECORATIVE PITCH PATTERNS

The "extra" pitches in melodies, which we call *decorative* or *embellishing pitches,* almost always bear a distinct and simple melodic relationship to their more basic neighbors. In Ex. 3, observe that the note *A* always occurs between the basic pitches *G* and *B*; it fills the gap between these two notes by providing a stepwise rise or fall from the one to the other.

Example 4

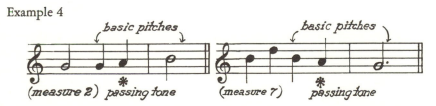

When a pitch fills the space between two basic pitches in this manner, it is called a *passing tone.* The melody shown in Ex. 1 contains several of these decorative tones, two of which are illustrated below.

Example 5

The passing-tone pattern is one of the simplest and most common connecting motions between any two basic pitches. There can, of course, be a pattern of more than one passing tone. Each of the melodic units below contains multiple passing tones.

Example 6

Another decorative pattern in melodies is the *neighboring tone*. Like the passing tone, the neighboring tone is a step above or below a basic pitch, but instead of linking two basic pitches, it returns to the same basic pitch. Each measure of Ex. 7 contains a neighboring-tone pattern.

Example 7

In some melodies a *double neighboring-tone* pattern (sometimes called a *changing tone* or *changing note* figure) occurs, with one decorative pitch followed by a second before a return to the basic pitch, as in the first and second measures below.

Example 8

Many melodies contain nothing more than three reference pitches—tonic, dominant, and mediant—and their *passing* or *neighboring* tones. We can develop fluency in recognizing and producing these pitches and the relationships between them by using the numbers 1 through 7 to denote them.

Sing each of the following patterns, making certain that the correct step relations are produced between the various pitches. Check with the piano if you are not sure at first. Before reading each line, carefully sing the pitches of the tonality frame for pitch orientation. Use the numbers or, if desired, *sol-fa* syllables as a text for your singing.

*PRACTICE PATTERNS*

These relationships sound the same, of course, when they are transposed to different pitch levels. The reader must learn to generalize pitch relationships so that he knows that the combinations of *C-G, G-D, E-B,* and so forth can all function in the same way as "tonic-dominant," "one-five," or *"do-sol."* This is the main reason for using numbers or *sol-fa* syllables rather than letter names for notes in early reading practice; the functional relations are the same for any pitch level.

Each of the following practice melodies has a tonality frame of a fifth or octave (tonic-dominant, tonic-tonic, or dominant-dominant) and decorative patterns restricted to passing tones and neighboring tones. Before singing each melody, circle the basic pitches lightly with pencil and identify as 1, 3, or 5 (or *do, mi, sol*). Then scan the melody to observe the relation of each decorative pitch to its more basic neighbors (neighboring tone above 5, passing tone between 3 and 5, and so forth). Sing only at a tempo that you can maintain with accuracy.

*PRACTICE MELODIES*

## MELODIES FROM LITERATURE

1. Guillaume d'Amiens

2. Guillaume d'Amiens

3. Schubert

*Andantino*

4. Prætorius

5. U.S.

6. Scarlatti

7. Beethoven

8. Hungary (Bartók)

9. Hayes

10. Haydn

11. Spain

12. Spain

13. Purcell

14. Germany

15. Hungary

16. Hungary

17. Spain

# 5

## SCALES

With the addition of passing and neighboring tones to the basic framework of tonic, dominant, and mediant tones, a relatively full roster of pitches becomes available for melodic reading. All of the pitches in any melody are conventionally represented by a *scale*. If we were to represent all of the pitches in "America" in order on the staff, from low to high, we would have a scalar representation of that melody's pitches.

Example 1    America

By convention, *scales* are usually notated in a definite way. For example, it is customary to show the tonic note as the lowest of the scale and to reduce all of the pitches to notes within a single octave, tonic-to-tonic. Example 2 shows the conventional scale representation for the pitches of "America."

Example 2    Scale for "America"

By using the same procedure for each of the following melodies, a scale can be derived that represents its pitches.

Example 3

(a)  Mozart

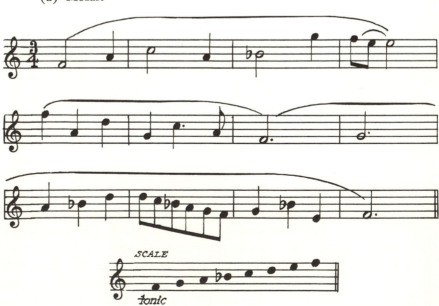

(b) Newfoundland

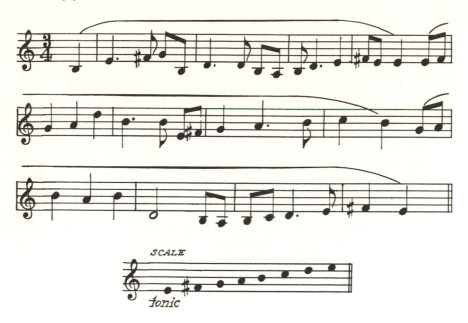

Many kinds of scales can act as the pitch bases for melodies. Some kinds that are more common in the music of our Western heritage have been classified according to the types of intervals which constitute them. Notice that the scales for melodies (a) and (b) above are different for two reasons: first, they have different tonics (*F* and *E*); second, there are different interval distances between some of their successive tones. Both scales have dominants a fifth above their respective tonics, but different mediants.

Example 4

Scale for 3 (a)

Scale for 3 (b)

An examination of successive intervals in these scales will reveal other differences.

Example 5

Scale (a)

Scale (b)

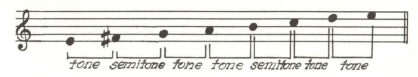

A scale that duplicated the interval relations of scale (a), but used *E* as tonic, would have to be written as in (c) below.

Example 6

Scale (c)

It would be possible to write some of these notes as flats; for example, the second note, *F#*, could be written enharmonically as *G♭* and still represent the correct pitch. However, it is a convention of musical notation that flats and sharps are not mixed in scales unless it is unavoidable, and that the successive letter names of the staff are not repeated or omitted in a scale unless absolutely necessary. A bit of experimentation with alternative spellings would show that both of these conventions cannot be met by any spelling except the one shown, *E-F#-G#-A-B-C#-D#-E.*

## THE MAJOR SCALE

Perhaps the easiest scale to sing—and certainly one of the most evident in the music of our common repertoire—is the *major scale*. Scales (a) and (c) above are major scales, consisting of whole-tone steps between all successive scale members except 3–4 and 7–8, which are semitone steps. It would be well, of course, to memorize the interval succession of any scale type dealt with. However, a more logical beginning can be made by learning any scale's three most significant characteristics. For the major scale, these are

1. *Dominant* a perfect fifth above (or fourth below) tonic.

2. *Mediant* a major third above tonic.

3. *Seventh tone* a semitone below tonic. (This forms a *leading-tone* relation to tonic.)

Each of the scales below satisfies all three of these most significant characteristics of major scales.

Example 7

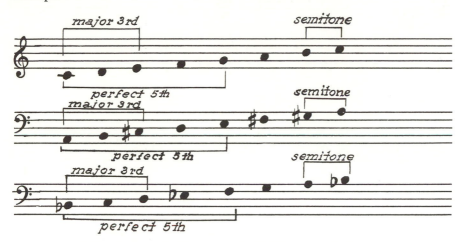

The presence of these three characteristics alone does not ensure that a scale is major, however. Three additional characteristics must be present for a scale to be major:

1. *Second degree* one whole tone above tonic.

2. *Fourth degree* one semitone above the mediant.

3. *Sixth degree* one whole tone above dominant.

Any scale comprised of these six relationships and these alone is a major scale. Following the process just described (satisfy the first three characteristics and then the second three characteristics), construct major scales above each of the tonics below. (A sample construction is shown first.)

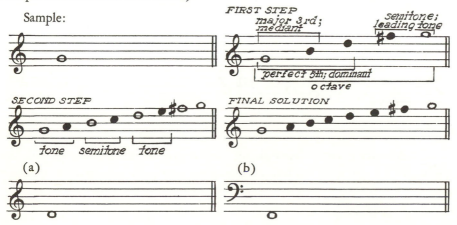

After completing the problem above correctly, determine which of the following scales are major. A scale that is not major can simply be marked X for the present.

It is important to learn all six pitch degrees of the major scale in relation to the tonic. To this end, the following patterns should be sung until committed to memory.

1. Sing 1 (any given tonic pitch), 5, 6, 5, 1.

example: [1]

2. Sing 1, 3, 4, 3, 1.

example:

3. Sing 1, 8 (octave above), 7, 8, 1.

example:

4. Sing any given tonic; then in slow, steady tempo sing other scale degrees at random, using appropriate numbers or *sol-fa* syllables. (In class, the teacher can point to each successive scale degree desired, if the scale is notated on the chalkboard.)

5. Sing each of the following pitch patterns in a steady tempo. Sing the appropriate degree number (or *sol-fa* syllable) for each pitch. Use any pitch as tonic.

---

[1] The sign ⌢ is called a *fermata* or *hold*. It indicates that the duration of the note below is prolonged past the usual designated time, for a period determined by the performer or conductor.

*THE MINOR SCALES*

The second scale type that serves as the pitch basis for a great number of melodies differs from the major in one very significant respect: its mediant degree is a *minor* third above tonic rather than a *major* third.

Example 8     Minor scale (natural form)

There are three forms of minor scales—*natural, harmonic,* and *melodic.* All have in common the minor mediant, but the interval structure of each distinguishes it from the others.

Example 9     (1 = whole tone; ½ = semitone)

(a) *Natural* minor

(b) *Harmonic* minor

(c) *Melodic* minor

(Notice that scale (b) mixes sharps and flats, thereby contradicting the notational convention mentioned earlier.)

Each form of minor differs from the others, then, only in the intervals formed between the fifth, sixth, seventh, and eighth notes of the scale. Notice also that the melodic form is a duplicate of the major scale except for the minor rather than major mediant.

For the present we shall deal with pitch patterns and melodies based on only the *natural* minor scale. In terms of its three basic characteristics, the natural minor scale differs from the major in two main ways: first, it contains a minor mediant; second, its seventh degree lies a whole tone rather than semitone below tonic, and is therefore known as a *subtonic* rather than a leading tone. Like the major scale, its dominant lies a perfect fifth above tonic.

Example 10

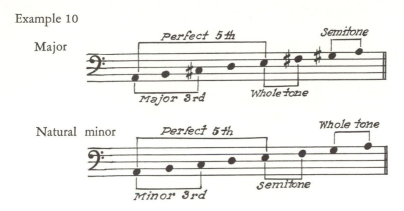

Its other main distinguishing feature is a sixth degree a semitone rather than a whole tone above the dominant.

Name each of the following scales.

The various degrees of the minor scale should be learned in relation to tonic in the same way that the major was learned in the previous section. The following patterns are duplicates of those on page 65 except that they are based on a minor rather than a major scale. These patterns should be studied diligently now and later returned to for practice.

1. Sing 1 (any given tonic pitch), 5, 6, 5, 1.

2. Sing 1, 3, 4, 3, 1.

3. Sing 1, 8, 7, 8, 1.

4. Sing any given tonic, then in slow, steady tempo sing other scale degrees at random, using appropriate numbers or *sol-fa* syllables.

5. Sing each of the following pitch patterns in a steady tempo. Sing the appropriate number (or *sol-fa* syllable) for each pitch. Use any pitch as tonic.

Like the first, third, fifth, and seventh notes (*tonic, mediant, dominant,* and *leading tone* or *subtonic*) of any scale, the remaining degrees have special names. The names below apply to any major or minor scale.

| Scale degree | Functional name |
|---|---|
| 1 | tonic |
| 2 | supertonic (note above tonic) |
| 3 | mediant |
| 4 | subdominant (dominant below tonic) |
| 5 | dominant |
| 6 | submediant (mediant below tonic) |
| 7 | leading tone (or subtonic) |

Since these names are used interchangeably with scale-degree numbers and *sol-fa* syllables, they should be memorized for future reference.

## KEYS AND KEY SIGNATURES

A melody based on a given scale is said to be *in the key of* that scale. For example, a melody whose basic scale is major with a tonic of *A* is said to be "in the key of *A* major"; a melody based on the scale of *D* minor is said to be "in the key of *D* minor." Thus two attributes are encompassed by the term "key": *tonic* and *scale type*.

Melodies based on a major or minor scale are usually notated in a way that makes them easier to read as well as easier to write. Using a *key signature* at the left side of any staff line simplifies the reading and writing of music; sharped or flatted notes need not be marked every time they appear. The alterations shown in a key signature prevail for the entire line of music, unless cancelled by a natural ( ♮ ), flat, or sharp sign within an individual measure. (When this happens, the cancellation affects only the measure in which it occurs and the notes in the octave in which it occurs.)

Example 11(b) shows the melody of 11(a) as it is written with a key signature.

Example 11
(a) Germany

(b)

The key signature generally is a clue that can be used to determine the key of a melody. A key signature of two sharps, for example, indicates that the melody is probably in the key of *D* major or *B* minor, for both of those scales require two sharps to create their natural forms.[2]

Example 12

*D* major:                                          *B* minor:

A key signature of two flats indicates that the key is probably *B*♭ major or *G* minor.

Example 13

*B*♭ major:                                          *G* minor:

The placement of sharps or flats in a key signature follows a set pattern. Example 14 shows the arrangement of sharps and flats for the two signatures that indicate the alteration of all natural notes.

Example 14

*C* ♯ major

*C* ♭ major

---

[2] The harmonic and melodic forms of minor scales, discussed earlier, are regarded as *altered* scales. Thus the key signatures for minor keys are based on the natural minor scale.

This arrangement is determined by the order in which natural notes must be altered to create major or minor scales. The *C* major and *A* minor scales require no alterations.

Example 15

The first sharp that is added to the set of natural notes to create another major scale is *F♯*. Rearranging the notes in proper succession produces the scales of *G* major and *E* minor.

Example 16

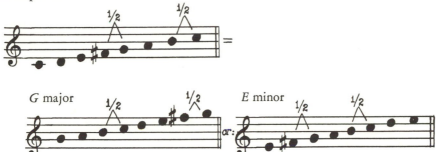

The first flat that is added to the set of natural notes to form a major or minor scale is *B♭*; the scales created are *F* major and *D* minor.

Example 17

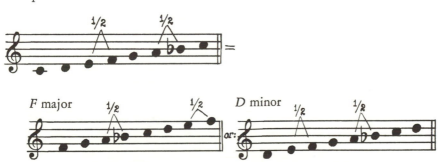

As Ex. 14 indicates, *F♯* is followed by *C♯*, *G♯*, *D♯*, *A♯*, *E♯*, and *B♯*; *B♭* is followed by *E♭*, *A♭*, *D♭*, *G♭*, *C♭*, and *F♭*. As above, the resultant scales can be found by arranging the half and whole tones in their proper order.

The melodies that follow are all based on major or minor scales. Like the melodies at the end of Chapter 4, they all are based solidly on simple tonality frames made up of some combination of tonic, dominant, or mediant. Some contain basic pitches other than tonic, dominant, and mediant, however. Before singing each melody, follow the procedure outlined below:

1. Determine the tonality frame and sing its constituent pitches. (Refer to a piano or pitch pipe for the tonic note.)

2. Determine scale type and sing from tonic to tonic, ascending and descending.

3. Scan the melody to find the basic pitches and decorative patterns (passing- or neighboring-tone patterns only).

4. Beat a regular tempo for one or more measures.

If any passage is particularly faulty, sing its pitches *without rhythm*, using numbers or *sol-fa* syllables.

## PRACTICE MELODIES

## MELODIES FROM LITERATURE

1. U.S.

2. Beethoven

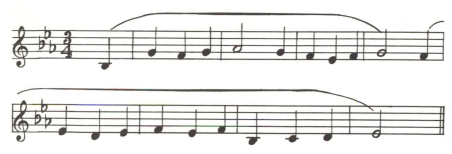

3. Chile

4. Verdi

5. Mozart

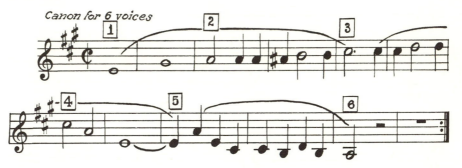

6. Prætorius

7. U.S.

8. Sweden

9. Arcadelt

10. U.S.

11. U.S.

12. Traditional carol

13. Germany (chorale)

14. Schubert

15. Bach

16. Germany (chorale)

17. England

18. Cavalli

19. Brahms

20. Bach

21. U.S.

22. Purcell

23. Sweden

24. Scarlatti

25. Germany

26. Gretry

27. Handel

28. Hungary (Bartók)

29. Handel

30. France

31. Schubert

32. Protestant hymn (Giardini)

33. U.S.

34. U.S.

35. U.S.

36. Hungary (Bartók)

37. Hungary (Kodály)

38. France

39. Billings

# 6

## SUBDIVISIONS OF THE BASIC DURATION IN SIMPLE METERS; C CLEFS

### SUBDIVISIONS IN SIMPLE METERS

Although a basic duration can be split into a limitless number of parts, musical notation is usually confined to a relatively limited set of note values. For example, many compositions written with a basic duration of a quarter note use only half, quarter, and eighth notes.

The basic durations of simple meters can be

divided into four equal parts as well as two. The notations of these subdivisions follow:

It is simplest to conceive of this subdivision pattern as four equal divisions of a single unit. Initially, it helps to emphasize the beginning of each basic duration by slightly stressing the first note of each four-part group, though this practice should not be continued after the subdivisions have become familiar.

Practice the rhythms below, using any syllable that you can articulate with ease. Be sure to make all double or quadruple divisions even. If "la-la-la-la" is not comfortable, try "ta-ta-ta-ta." For extremely rapid practice, the pattern "ka-ta-ka-ta" or "ta-ka-ta-ka" can be useful.[1]

*PRACTICE PATTERNS*

The subdivision patterns above divide the basic duration into four notes of equal length. Once this four-part division can be read with some fluency, it is easy to learn combinations of the subdivisions. The following combinations occur frequently in music.

---

[1] The student or teacher can devise other syllable patterns that reflect the stressed and unstressed parts of the basic duration. "Ka-fa-ke-fa" and "ka-ta-ke-ta" are two possibilities that may be helpful.

SUBDIVISION COMBINATIONS

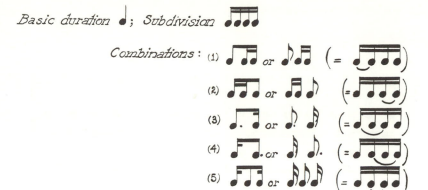

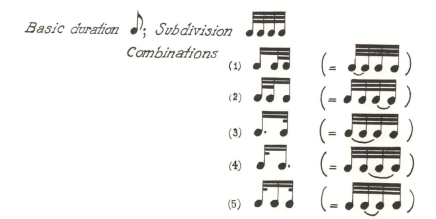

For practice in reading subdivisions, use arrangements such as the following. Each pattern consists of two full measures of a duple-simple meter. Begin with the top line of each grouping and move down, or skip randomly from one line to another, always maintaining a steady tempo.[2] The colon sign (:‖) at the end of a pattern indicates that the whole pattern is to be repeated.

*PRACTICE PATTERNS*

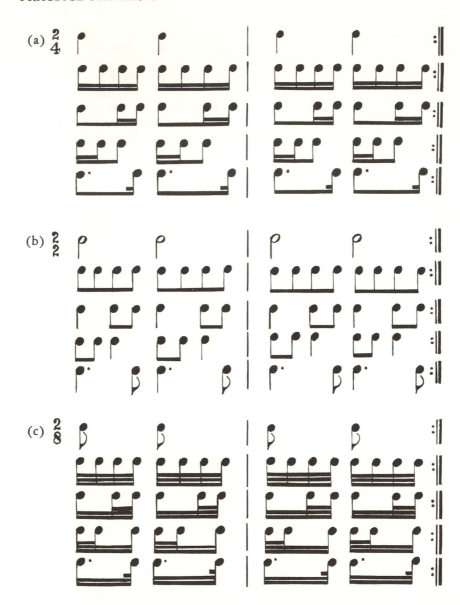

The melodies that follow contain no new problems except subdivision patterns. After developing some fluency in reading these melodies, write similar examples of your own, incorporating subdivisions of the basic duration. Play or sing these for

---

[2] In a class, the instructor can indicate the line to be read by pointing to a diagram notated on the chalkboard.

fellow students to write down. When giving a dictation problem, name the meter and key and play the pitches of the tonality frame, naming each as *tonic, dominant,* or *mediant.* Establish the pulse for two measures before beginning your performance.

*PRACTICE MELODIES*

## TRIPLETS IN SIMPLE METERS

The basic duration of a simple meter is frequently divided into triplets. Because this is not the normal division, it usually is marked with a triplet sign.

$$\ulcorner 3 \urcorner \quad \text{or} \quad \widehat{3}$$

(The three-part division of a basic duration is normal for compound meters, which we shall discuss in Chapter 8.)

In performing triplets in a normally duplet context, take care to divide the basic duration into three equal parts. It is easy to misread the triplet as some combination of two-part divisions. The following examples show errors that sometimes occur when a reader is not careful.

Example 1

*Incorrect versions:*

These incorrect readings can be avoided by taking care to develop the feeling of a three-part division of the basic duration. The following exercise is useful. Read it slowly the first time, and increase the tempo with each repetition, making sure that you always divide the basic duration into equal thirds.

Example 2

Once the triplet division is easy to perform with fluency, read the following rhythms at a steady tempo. Clap, tap, or conduct the basic pulse for each exercise while singing "la" for the written rhythm.

*PRACTICE PATTERNS*

(e)

(f)

(g)

All of the melodies that follow use triplets in a simple meter. If reading is difficult at first, practice just the rhythm before attempting to sing the melody.

*PRACTICE MELODIES*

(a)

(b)

(c)

(d)

(i)

## THE C CLEFS, ALTO AND TENOR

Although the *C* clef was mentioned in Chapter 2, all previous melodic examples have been notated in the more familiar treble and bass clefs. Like the bass and treble clefs, the *C* clef locates a certain note (middle *C* or $c^1$) on the musical staff; unlike them, it can be shifted to locate middle *C* on different lines of the staff. In modern notation this clef is usually limited to two different locations, as shown below.

Example 3

The *treble clef* locates $g^1$ on the second staff line

The *bass clef* locates $f$ on the fourth staff line

The *alto clef* locates middle *C* on the middle staff line

The *tenor clef* locates middle *C* on the fourth staff line

This renaming of the lines and spaces of the staff is confusing at first for the reader who is accustomed to the treble and bass clefs. For this reason, the initial practice melodies in the new *C* clefs are quite simple. You should never translate the new note

designations into treble or bass clefs, for this translation process is a crutch that is not easily discarded. Since the new *C* clefs are a significant hurdle after you have developed fluency in the more familiar clefs, you should study this chapter until you can read notes in the *C* clef with some fluency before moving on to the next chapter.

Recite the preparatory studies that follow slowly at first, using only the *spoken* note names. It is important to keep a strict tempo throughout the reading in order to force a habit of immediate recall. Once you can recite the pattern as a spoken line, follow the same procedure again, singing the correct pitches. (Still use the note names.) If possible, play each pattern on an instrument (preferably the piano) to bring about a mechanical association with the new clef.

*PRACTICE PATTERNS, ALTO CLEF*

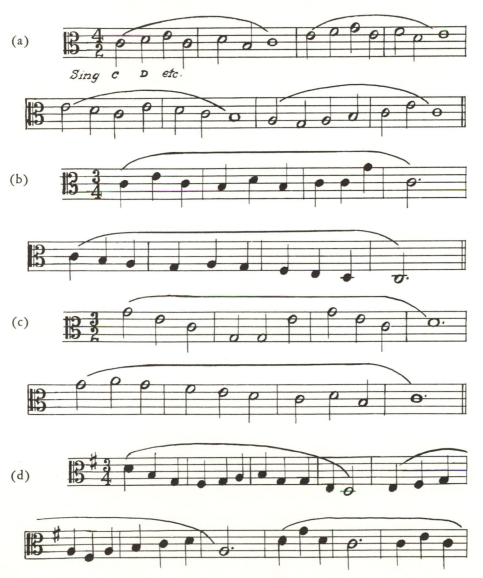

*PRACTICE PATTERNS, TENOR CLEF*

# *MELODIES FROM LITERATURE*

1. Beethoven

2. U.S.

3. Schumann

4. Paumann

5. U.S.

6. Rameau

7. U.S.

8. U.S.

9. Verdi

10. Mexico

11. U.S.

**12. U.S.**

**13. Weber**

14. U.S.

15. Schubert

16. Schubert

17. Mozart

18. U.S.

19. Mozart

20. Rameau

21. Handel

22. France

23. U.S.

24. U.S.

25. Finland

26. U.S.

27. U.S.

28. Germany

29. France

30. U.S.

31. Canada

32. Handel

33. Ireland

34. Scotland

35. Schumann

36. Lully

37. Ireland

38. Mendelssohn

39. U.S.

40. England

41. Gretry

42. Gluck

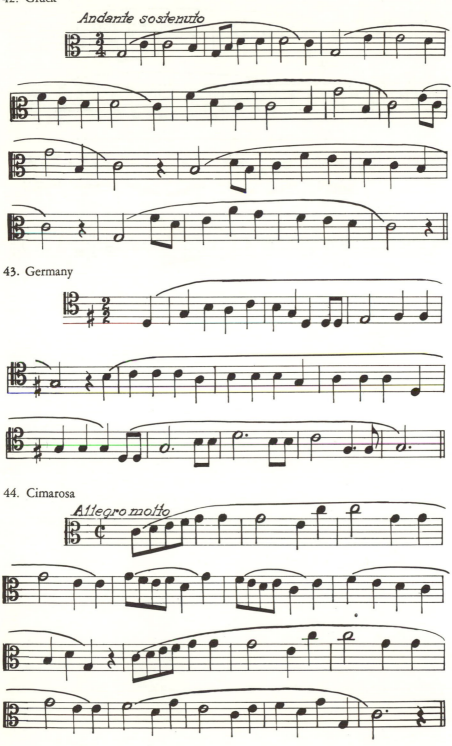

43. Germany

44. Cimarosa

45. Mozart

# 7

## *MELODIC FORM*

### *PHRASE STRUCTURE*

Most of the melodies in the foregoing chapters have been notated with phrase marks—long curved lines that designate natural divisions in the patterns of the melody. Phrase marks are helpful in reading music because they divide the melody into shorter units and indicate the points where one can breathe (in some instances with extreme haste!) without destroying the natural flow of the line.

Just as an experienced reader of prose or poetry reads "by sentences" rather than by separate words (or letters), an experienced music reader "reads by phrases"; that is, he thinks of the notes of a melody as groups rather than individual notes. A melodic phrase is roughly the equivalent of a sentence; it represents a musical statement that has a certain degree of completeness and seems to be set off from other groups of notes.

The division of the melody below into phrases is easy to see, because each phrase is separated from the others by a brief silence.

Example 1      Saint-Saëns

Notice that the melody has seven sections, each clearly delineated by periods of silence. This melody is unified by its adherence to a single tonic and scale (*F* major) and by the rhythmic similarity of its parts. Notice the pattern of unity and variety established by the repetition and contrast of the phrases. The first four phrases are based on a single rhythmic pattern,

while the last three phrases move, for the most part, in different quarter-note patterns. As a whole, this melody exemplifies a successful organization of musical tones—it has *form*. We can diagram its organization by using letters to represent its parts:

$$\overset{\displaystyle \mathbf{A}}{\underbrace{a \quad a' \quad a'' \quad a'''}} \quad \overset{\displaystyle \mathbf{B}}{\underbrace{b \quad b' \quad b''}}$$

(The superscripts denote some alteration of the original pattern.)

To read a melody fluently, a performer must know something about its organization. A careful reader scans a melody before performing it, to determine several important characteristics which will aid him:

1. Length.

2. Approximate number and relative lengths of phrases.

3. Repeated pitch or rhythm patterns.

4. General pitch contour of each phrase (rising, falling, stationary).

5. Basic pitches in each phrase.

6. Possible reading difficulties.

The Saint-Saëns melody above has two sections, the second a slight contrast to the first; thus it has a two-part or *binary* form. In melodies such as the above, several similar phrases constitute each section; in other melodies, sections may be no longer than a single phrase.

Many folk and "popular" melodies follow a different basic plan. As in the binary form, a main pattern is followed by a contrasting pattern; however, this contrasting section leads to the return of the main section. This three-part or *ternary* form, which is used in the songs below, is diagrammed as A B A. (The repeated "A" in the beginning section is regarded as only half of the total section; this form is sometimes diagrammed as A :‖ B A and called *rounded binary* form.)

Example 2

    (a) Germany

    (b) Germany

In the first melody, the two phrases of the first section are the same in the beginning but slightly different at the end. The entire section is therefore called a *parallel period*. In many melodies of similar structure, the contrast between the ends of the two phrases is greater than in this melody, but if the phrases begin in the same way, they still constitute a parallel period.

Since the first section of melody (b), Ex. 2, begins with a section composed of identical phrases, it is not a true parallel period, but a *repeated phrase*. (Note that since the final section A is the same as the first two, the reader can perform three-fourths of the melody when he has mastered the first four measures!)

A third kind of section, made up of phrases which are not similar enough to classify as identical in any way, is known as a *phrase group*. The melody shown below is a good illustration. Since the four phrases are all quite similar in rhythm, but different enough in pitch structure to be regarded as separate sections of the melody, they constitute a phrase group.

Example 3       U.S.

The well-known tune "Silent Night" is a slightly more complex example of a phrase group.

Example 4       Silent Night   (Gruber)

## MOTIVES

The phrases in most melodies are themselves made up of smaller structural units, called *motives* or *figures*. Hum or sing through "Silent Night" and then study the melodic analysis below.

Example 5      Silent Night

In "Silent Night," a few basic patterns are repeated and varied to create the melodic line. Motive "a" is particularly conspicuous, for its dotted rhythm reappears as a part of other motives (in the fifth, sixth, seventh, eighth, ninth, and eleventh measures), binding the melody together.

Like the phrase, the motive does not have a fixed length; it consists of the smallest number of tones that can be regarded as a single melodic unit. In cases where the motive is as long as the phrase, there is no reason to differentiate one from the other.

Melodic lines are frequently derived from one main rhythm repeated several times in the same form or with slight variations. Once the reader becomes familiar with this dominating pattern, the whole melody is much easier to perform. The main pattern of the next melody is established in the first two measures; nothing really new—in terms of rhythm—occurs in the rest of the song, for the other patterns are clearly related to the first. Notice that the third phrase consists of a sequence built from the second measure's rhythm. (Sequences are discussed below.)

Example 6     Germany

The next melody is more tightly unified around a single motive than most; half of it is based on the single rhythmic figure with which it begins.

Example 7     Pachelbel

One typical way that a repeated motive is spun out deserves special attention: repeating a motive on a different pitch level is a particularly effective way of creating melodic unity. This procedure results in a *sequence,* or *sequential organization.*

Example 8     Mozart

Even if each pattern is not an exact duplicate of the one before, the term "sequence" still applies. In the next melody, for example, most of the second half is a sequence, although patterns 2 and 3 do not begin exactly as pattern 1 does.

Example 9     Wales

In this sequence, the pitch line moves down one scale step with each repetition. Notice that this creates a simple basic-pitch outline, which begins with the dominant (E♭) in measure 9 and successively steps down through D♭, C, and B♭, reaching the tonic, A♭, in the last three measures.

All sequences do not move by step motion, however. The following melody begins with a motive that returns in sequence a fourth lower, followed in turn by a motive that is repeated in sequence a step higher.

Example 10     Germany

When the pitch modifications in a repeated motive or phrase are extensive, the term *modified sequence* is sometimes used. But since this terminology can result in mere hair-splitting, "sequence" is usually employed to describe any series of patterns having the same rhythm and general pitch contours.

## MELODIC CADENCES

When we speak, our voices produce various patterns—rise and fall, slow and fast, hard accent and soft accent. All of these articulations transmit our ideas more effectively; they help to produce the movement and repose of our phrases and sentences. Without them, our speech would be a stream of uncommunicative boredom. Music, like language, has points of repose, which punctuate and give form to tonal patterns. A cadence is a musical "signal" of relative degrees of melodic repose; it separates one phrase from another, creating an effect similar to that of commas and colons and periods in written language.

We can name cadences according to their roles in a melody. For the present, we shall deal only with the two most fundamental types; these can be deduced from melody alone, without bothering about the harmonies that might be associated with them. The first, the *terminal cadence,* indicates a complete or relatively complete cessation of melodic activity. A phrase that ends with a certain degree of finality ends with a terminal cadence. The second, called a *progressive cadence,* implies that the melodic activity will continue. The parallel period form reproduced below illustrates both kinds of melodic punctuation. Sing this melody to observe the cadences that close the two phrases.

Example 11

The progressive cadence that ends phrase A gives no feeling that the melody could end there; on the contrary, one feels that the melody must be continued. But the cadence for phrase A' ends with the tonic pitch, and signals a potential end to melodic activity. The melody may not actually end with this cadence, but it *could end* with relative satisfaction: the cadence is terminal in effect.

Different degrees of finality can be suggested by different terminal cadences. The most final is a cadence pattern in which the last note is both the tonic pitch and a metric accent. In some contexts, however, other members of the tonic chord can also have the effect of finality that characterizes a terminal cadence. If a cadential pattern outlines the tonic chord, the dominant or the mediant pitches can also produce a terminal cadence, although their effect will be less final than that of the tonic. The melody below contains two terminal cadences—the first on the mediant (*E*), the second on the tonic (*C*).

Example 12

Most simple melodies that begin with two parallel phrases have a progressive cadence at the end of the first phrase and a terminal cadence at the end of the second. This arrangement ensures a continued thrust from the first phrase to the second, for the progressive cadence demands continued motion. The following melody is a classic example of this form. The first cadence is made on the supertonic pitch, *D*, the second on the tonic pitch, *C*.

Example 13    Scotland

In certain other melodies of the same form, both parallel phrases end with terminal cadences.

All of the following melodies have relatively simple formal plans. Study them and mark their phrase structure and cadence types before singing. Although it is not essential to mark motives and sequences, take note of them and bear them in mind as you sing.

# MELODIES FROM LITERATURE

1. U.S.

2. Sullivan

3. Bach

4. Saint-Saëns

5. Handel

6. Handel

**7. Scarlatti**

**8. Hungary (Kodály)**

**9. Schubert**

**10. Canada**

11. Brazil

12. Smetana

13. Mozart

14. Mozart

15. Tchaikovsky

16. Dvořák

17. Ireland

18. Brahms

19. Purcell

20. Wales

21. Scotland

22. Haydn

23. Donizetti

24. Brahms

25. Bach

# 8

## COMPOUND METERS

### DOTTED-NOTE BASIC DURATIONS
### AND THEIR SIMPLEST DIVISIONS

When the basic duration of a melody is consistently divided into triplets, a *compound meter* (as opposed to a simple meter) is established. The triplet division is already familiar in simple meters, where it is marked by the triplet sign.

For ease and logic of notation, compound meters use dotted-note values for their basic durations. By eliminating the need for the triplet sign, this practice indicates that a three-part division is natural in these meters. For example, in $\frac{6}{8}$ the dotted quarter note divides evenly into three eighth notes, and in $\frac{6}{4}$ the dotted half divides evenly into three quarter notes. The following table of first-order divisions and multiples in the usual compound meters should be memorized.

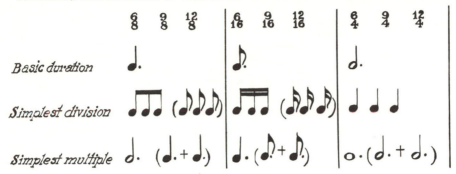

In the example below, note that the same rhythm can be notated in a simple or compound meter.

Example 1

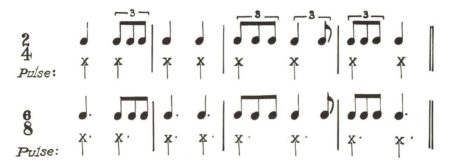

Most melodies are organized around a characteristic pattern—a motive in some cases—that is repeated frequently. The characteristic pattern might be the simplest division of the meter's basic duration, as in (a) below, or some combination of the divisions of the basic duration, as in (b) and (c).

Example 2

(a)

Scanning the melody to find these repetitions of a rhythmic pattern reduces the problem of performing a melody considerably; directing your attention to *combinations* rather than isolated notes, by observing characteristic patterns such as these, leads to more fluent performance.

It is necessary to learn that no note value means anything unless it is placed in some metric context. In $\frac{6}{8}$ time, for example, the dotted half note represents two beats, in $\frac{6}{4}$ it represents only one beat, and in $\frac{3}{4}$ it represents three beats. The difficulty which beginning readers sometimes have in learning this can be overcome only with experience.

Practice the rhythms below until you can read them fluently.

*PRACTICE PATTERNS*

## REST SIGNS IN COMPOUND METERS

The rest signs in compound meters are the same as those learned for simple meters, and the whole rest still represents a full measure of silence. Two conventions affecting the use of rests in compound meters merit special attention, however.

1. Some writers do not use the dotted quarter rest for a full basic duration of silence; they insist upon a quarter and an eighth rest. For example, they would use (a) rather than (b) below, although either is quite correct.

Example 3

In $\frac{6}{4}$ or $\frac{9}{4}$, they would use a half and a quarter rest, rather than a dotted half rest. (This book uses both kinds of notation.)

2. To make reading easier, rests are always positioned to reveal the beat structure of the measure. For example, (a), (b), (c), and (d) below all contain the proper number of notes and rests, but (b) and (d) conceal the distribution of beats in the measure.

Example 4

## CONDUCTING PATTERNS FOR COMPOUND METERS

Unless the tempo is extremely slow, music in a compound meter can be conducted with the same hand patterns used for simple meters having the same number of beats. For instance, $\frac{6}{8}$ or $\frac{6}{4}$ meter is conducted with the same two-beat pattern used for $\frac{2}{8}$, $\frac{2}{4}$, or $\frac{2}{2}$ (Ex. 5).

Example 5

The conducting pattern used for triple-simple meters ($\frac{3}{8}$, $\frac{3}{4}$, $\frac{3}{2}$) is used for compound meters such as $\frac{9}{8}$, $\frac{9}{4}$, or $\frac{9}{16}$.

Example 6

The four-beat pattern is used for conducting quadruple-compound as well as simple meters.

Example 7.

Hand motion

Rhythm $\frac{12}{8}$

A basic pattern can be used in reading whenever the tempo of a melody is not so slow that it would be cumbersome.[1] Such patterns should be used to ensure a steady

---

[1] In music of decidedly slow tempo it frequently aids both the conductor and the performer if a *divided* conducting pattern is used. Such a pattern shows the simple division of the basic duration as well as the basic metric structure. The student who is just learning to read music will find these divided patterns of more hindrance than help, since they consist of such complex hand motions that they are of little value as an aid to rhythmic scansion. They may be found in any book on elementary conducting.

rhythm and a feeling for its movement. When you can beat a steady conducting pattern without conscious effort, you will find that this hand motion forces you to articulate the rhythms accurately. When difficulties of pitch reading arise, however, it is usually better just to tap a hand or foot temporarily, so that you can pay undivided attention to the immediate difficulty.

      The following practice melodies contain the most common patterns in the compound meters. Regard each new melody as a fresh problem in musical analysis, and continue singing tonality frames and basic scales for preliminary pitch orientation.

### PRACTICE MELODIES

(m)

## MELODIES FROM LITERATURE

1. U.S.

2. U.S.

3. Ireland

4. Donizetti

5. U.S.

**6. Schubert**

**7. Mendelssohn**

**8. Gluck**

9. Schumann

10. Bizet

11. Beethoven

12. Germany

13. France

14. Traditional

15. England

16. France

17. Beethoven

18. Scotland

19. Schubert

20. Spain

21. Mozart

22. Couperin

23. England

24. Wales

25. Haydn

26. Telemann

27. Offenbach

28. England

29. Canada

# 9

## TWO OTHER MINOR SCALES; TRANSIENT-TERMINAL CADENCES

In Chapter 5 only one scale containing the minor third as mediant was introduced: the *natural* minor scale. This form is no more prevalent in melodies than the two discussed below; it was introduced first only because it differs so markedly from the major scale that it offers a simpler example of a contrasting scale.

## HARMONIC MINOR

The other two minor scales can be regarded as altered versions of the natural minor. One, the so-called *harmonic* minor,[1] differs from the natural minor only in that its seventh degree is a semitone higher, creating a leading-tone relation to tonic.

Example 1

Notice that raising the seventh note a half step also creates a new interval, the *augmented second,* between the sixth and seventh scale degrees. (Any major interval, when altered to be a semitone larger, becomes an *augmented interval.*)

The harmonic minor scale can be learned more easily by temporarily ignoring the augmented second between 6 and 7 as such. Instead, begin with the more basic pitches 5 and 8, and learn 6 and 7 in relation to them, as the following example demonstrates.

Example 2

SING: "one-five-eight-five-one"; "six-five"; "seven-eight"; "five-six-seven-eight — one"

Perform this same exercise in other keys, using pitch letter names rather than scale-degree numbers or *sol-fa* syllables, as in the following example in *B* minor:

Example 3

SING: "B - F sharp-B - F sharp - B"; "G - F sharp; A sharp-B"; "F sharp-G-A sharp-B - B"

Sing each of the following practice patterns in two different ways, until you have learned it thoroughly: (1) using scale-degree numbers or *sol-fa* syllables, and (2) using pitch letter names (always naming the required sharp or flat). Sing each pattern in every key, shifting octaves when your comfortable singing range is exceeded.

---

[1] The name "harmonic minor" is used because, presumably, the scale was derived from a chordal (*harmonic*) pattern with which it is associated. A discussion of this origin is not germane here.

PRACTICE PATTERNS

## MELODIC MINOR

The third minor scale is known as the *melodic minor*. It can be regarded as a natural minor scale with its sixth and seventh degrees raised one half step.

Example 4

Notice that the melodic minor scale is like the major scale except for its mediant, which is a *minor* third rather than a *major* third above tonic.

The following patterns can be used to learn melodic minor scales. Transpose to different keys and sing with pitch letter names, numbers, and (optionally) *sol-fa* syllables.

PRACTICE PATTERNS

In reading melodies that obviously are minor (because they contain a minor mediant above tonic), you can usually recognize the harmonic and melodic scale types with ease, because certain accidentals appear in the melody. Since the key signatures for minor keys are based upon natural scales, the sixth and seventh degrees must be raised for the melodic minor, while the seventh degree is raised for the harmonic minor. It is quite common to find two of these scales side by side, and in some rare instances all three scales occur in a single melody.

In many melodies, an ascending passage using the melodic form is followed by a descending passage based on the natural form. Since this pattern occurs so frequently, many musicians have considered the melodic minor an ascending scale, the natural minor its descending counterpart.

Example 5

There are exceptions to this general rule, however; the melodic minor sometimes occurs in descending passages.

The melodies at the end of this chapter contain the various rhythm and pitch materials that we have covered, including compound meters and the harmonic and melodic forms of the minor scale. Before singing, always analyze the form, tonality frame, dominating rhythms, and scale form of each melody.

## TRANSIENT-TERMINAL CADENCES

The two most basic cadences, *terminal* and *progressive,* were introduced in Chapter 7. Now that all the pitches in the chromatic scale have been introduced, we can discuss a third kind of cadence, which resembles both the terminal and progressive types; we shall call it a *transient-terminal* cadence.[2] It establishes a temporary sense of finality in a melody, on some pitch other than tonic; however, this apparent termination is denied by a clear reaffirmation of the original tonic.

In the fifth and sixth measures of the following example, the melody hovers around *C* in a way that causes this pitch to act as a new point of focus; it seems to have replaced *F* as tonic.

Example 6    Dunstable

---

[2] See Christ *et al., Materials and Structures of Music* (Englewood Cliffs, N. J.: Prentice-Hall, Inc., 1966), pp. 56–58.

If the melody ended at the sixth measure, there would be good reason to think that it began in the key of *F* and ended in the key of *C*; a *modulation*, or change of tonic, would have occurred.[3] But since the melody clearly reaffirms *F* as tonic, the fifth and sixth measures must be interpreted differently. In these measures, the fifth degree, *C*, is merely emphasized by its repetition and its chromatic embellishment, *B*-natural: it creates, therefore, a *transient-terminal* cadence.

It is usually easy to see transient-terminal cadences in a melody, because such melodies, like the one above, frequently contain a note that is raised by a half step to act as an embellishment of the temporary (or *transient*) tonic. (If this altered note persists in the measures that follow, a real change of key probably has occurred.)

Before attempting to perform each of the following melodies, scan it to determine where difficulties with pitch or rhythm might occur. When you find chromatic pitches,[4] determine their most obvious relation to the prevailing tonality frame member or other scale degree. If necessary, take the problematic pitch or rhythm pattern and practice it out of its context.

As a vocal exercise for developing a fluent recall of chromatic pitches in relation to a particular scale, the following practice format is helpful:

1. Establish a tonic pitch; sing 1–3–5–8–5–3–1 as a tonality frame.
2. Teacher requests: "Sing semitone below 6."
3. Class responds: "la" (on correct pitch)—"six" (on correct pitch).
4. Continue with requests for other embellishing relations, such as semitone below 5, semitone above 4.

*PRACTICE MELODIES*

(a)

(b)

---

[3] Modulation will be discussed further in Chapter 13.

[4] Pitches that are not members of the prevailing scale.

## MELODIES FROM LITERATURE

1. Dressler[5]

2. Mozart

3. Gluck

4. Bizet

[5] In $\frac{4}{2}$ meter, a complete measure's duration is represented by the *breve* (measure 9) which equals two whole notes. It is the longest note used in most modern notation, and occurs infrequently.

**5. Tchaikovsky**

**6. Krieger**

**7. Pergolesi**

8. Mozart

9. Tchaikovsky

10. Couperin

11. Massenet

12. Schubert

13. Brahms

14. Beethoven

15. Schubert

16. Russia

17. Boyce

18. Schubert

**19. Russian hymn**

**20. Mendelssohn**

**21. Schumann**

22. Gounod

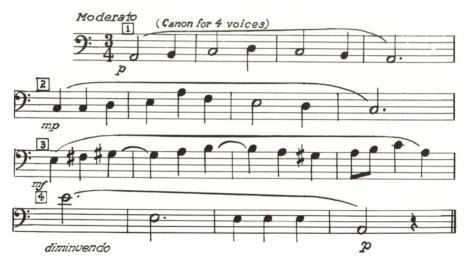

# 10

## *ADDITIONAL DECORATIVE PATTERNS; CHROMATIC EMBELLISHMENTS*

Thus far our melodies have contained only basic pitches and the patterns that are formed by passing and neighboring tones. These tonal patterns account for most melodic motion, since many songs contain nothing more in the way of pitch organization. In this chapter, we shall learn two other melodic patterns.

## THE LEANING-TONE PATTERN

The first additional decorative pattern consists of a tone that results from a skip and moves a step up or down to a more basic pitch.[1] The middle note is called a *leaning tone* because it "leans" toward its note of resolution. (The traditional name for this figure is "appoggiatura," but we shall adopt its less formidable English equivalent.)

Example 1

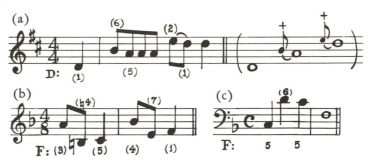

In reading such patterns, it is helpful to concentrate on the two outer tones of the three-note figure, thinking of the middle note in relation to the last note.

Example 2

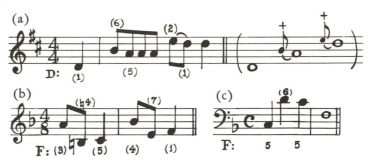

In most patterns of this kind, the middle tone resolves in the opposite direction from which it was approached. (In (b) above, for example, each leaning tone is approached by a leap down and resolved by a step up.) Some exceptions to this generalization are illustrated below.

Example 3

---

[1] In many melodic patterns, it is useless to call one pitch more basic than another, for all the pitches in a group may be of equal duration. In the melodies that follow in the "Practice Melodies" section, however, basic pitches will be clearly established by their greater duration. Even in patterns where all notes are equal, such as Ex. 1(d), we tend to regard the outer notes of each pattern as more basic than the inner note; thus these patterns are leaning-tone patterns.

## THE ESCAPE-TONE PATTERN

The opposite of the leaning-tone pattern is the *escape-tone* pattern, in which a step motion away from a basic pitch is followed by a skip to another basic pitch.[2]

Example 4

(a)

(b)

As with the leaning tone, it is easiest to think of the escape tone in relation to the basic pitch a step away from it.

## CHROMATIC EMBELLISHMENTS OF 5 AND 3

We have already encountered chromatic pitches in the discussions of transient-terminal cadences, leaning tones, and escape tones; we shall now learn all five chromatic pitches systematically, so that we can make use of all twelve pitches of the chromatic scale. We shall begin by learning nondiatonic pitches (notes not in the scale) as chromatic embellishments of familiar scale degrees.

Once you have memorized the tonic-dominant relationship, it is not difficult to use it as a reference in recalling other pitch relations. For example, the tonic-dominant relation in the key of $C$ ($C$-$G$) can serve as the basis of orientation for $C$-$F\sharp$ or $C$-$A\flat$, since $F\sharp$ is the lower chromatic inflection[3] of $G$, and $A\flat$ is its upper chromatic inflection.

Example 5

---

[2] You should remember that this analysis of basic and decorative pitches does not take into account any notion of implied or imposed harmonic background. In many cases, accompanying chords could reverse our designations of basic and decorative pitches.

[3] A *chromatic inflection* is any chromatic pitch related as upper or lower leading tone to any scale pitch.

The same chromatic inflections of the dominant apply, of course, in any key. In the key of *A* major, *D♯* is the lower inflection of the dominant, *E*, and *F* is its upper inflection; in the key of *B♭* major, *E* and *G♭* are the inflections of the dominant, *F*.

To gain familiarity with chromatic embellishments of the dominant, sing the following patterns in various keys, using note names. The minor pattern is limited to the lower chromatic embellishment, because the upper embellishment is a normal scale degree. (For example, *A♭* is the sixth degree of the natural and harmonic forms of the *C* minor scale.)

*PRACTICE PATTERNS*

Sing the same patterns in other major keys, using note names.

Sing the same pattern in other minor keys, using note names.

In major keys, the mediant can be embellished just as the dominant is in minor keys. The embellishing pitch is the same as the minor mediant, but in a major context it is best regarded as a pitch that is a semitone below the major mediant. This embellishment is illustrated below in *D* major. (Both notations of the embellishing tone occur in music, although *E♯* is favored.)

Example 6

Chromatically altered notes in melodies are not always embellishments of this sort. In some cases, an accidental results from an actual change of key (or *modulation*) in a melody; in other cases, the chromatic pitch does not resolve immediately to the scale tone it embellishes. In the passage below, for example, the melody drops from *G♯* to *D* before it reaches the dominant, *A,* in the following measure. When reading such passages of delayed resolution, you can still sing the chromatic pitch most accurately by mentally relating it to the dominant, or mediant.

Example 7

Since the pitch a semitone below 5 is also a semitone above 4 in major and minor scales (note that it can be written enharmonically as ♯4 or as ♭5), there are two possible ways of relating it to a known framework.

Example 8

The same duality of spelling and interpretation is true for the chromatic inflection of the mediant (3). In Ex. 6, *F♮* can also be interpreted as the upper inflection of 2, and *E♯* as the lower inflection of 3.

Example 9

The discussion has stressed these inflections in relation to the *dominant* and *mediant,* because these two degrees are easier to remember than any others of the scale except *tonic,* and they were learned as potential members of tonality frames. However, if your own ability or a particular melodic context makes an alternative interpretation more practical, then you should use it. The important thing is that you do relate the unknown pitch to some pitch that you already know.

The interval between the tonic and the lower chromatic embellishment of the dominant is not easy to sing unless the upper note is thought of in relation to the dominant. When this interval is notated as in Ex. 7, it is an *augmented fourth,* but it can be notated as a *diminished fifth* with equal logic (*D-A♭,* for example). Two intervals such as these, which contain the same pitches but are notated differently, are called *enharmonic intervals.* Each pair of intervals below is enharmonic.

Example 10      Enharmonic intervals

The diminished fifth and augmented fourth are unique intervals in that they are frequently given the same name, *tritone*—an appropriate name, because three (thus *tri-*) whole tones separate the two pitches in both intervals.

Example 11      Tritones

This same interval occurs between the fourth and seventh degrees of the major scale and the harmonic **and** melodic minor scales. It also occurs between the second and sixth degrees of the **natural and** harmonic minor scales, and between the third and sixth degrees of the melodic **minor scale**.

Example 12      Tritones in major and minor scales

The practice melodies that follow make exaggerated use of chromatic inflections of the dominant and mediant scale degrees. Before singing each, scan to determine the tonality frame. Then find the basic pitches to which melodic patterns, both diatonic and chromatic, can be related. If necessary, circle all the basic pitches in a melody lightly, with pencil, and indicate their location in the scale (5, 3, 7, etc.). After one or two readings, when the melody has become less problematic, erase these marks and sing the melody without them.

PRACTICE MELODIES

# MELODIES FROM LITERATURE

1. U.S.

2. Brahms

3. U.S.

4. U.S.

5. Tchaikovsky

6. U.S.

7. Bizet

8. Grieg

9. Schumann

10. Rossini

**11. Sweden**

**12. Schubert**

**13. Mozart**

14. Gounod

15. Beethoven

16. Fauré

17. Brahms

18. Bach

# 11

---

## SUBDIVISIONS IN COMPOUND METERS; FURTHER CHROMATIC EMBELLISHMENTS

---

### SUBDIVISIONS IN COMPOUND METERS

*Subdivisions* of the basic durations of compound meters are normally two-part divisions, as in simple meters. The diagram below shows the divisions and subdivisions for $\frac{6}{8}$ meter compared to those for $\frac{2}{4}$ meter.

*DIVISIONS OF THE BASIC DURATION IN* $\frac{2}{4}$ *AND* $\frac{6}{8}$

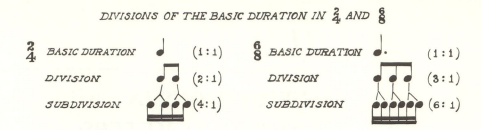

In compound meters as in simple meters, deviations from the ordinary divisions and subdivisions are notated with appropriate signs, as in the example below.

Example 1

In reading subdivisions, it is helpful, of course, to mentally keep track of the simple divisions as well as the basic duration. Without this orientation, the reader can lose track of the meter. As a preliminary exercise, practice the following pattern. Tap the basic pulse (top line) with your foot and the divisions with your hand, and sing the subdivisions (bottom line) on a single pitch, using "ta-da, ta-da, ta-da," or "la-la, la-la, la-la."

Example 2

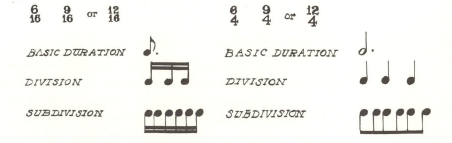

The diagram below shows the notation of subdivisions in the other usual compound meters.

*SUBDIVISIONS IN COMPOUND METERS*

Practice the following passages over a period of at least several days (returning to them after you have studied subsequent parts of this chapter). Tap the pulse with your hand until your reading is relatively fluent, then use the appropriate conducting pattern.

### PRACTICE PATTERNS

## CHROMATIC EMBELLISHMENTS OF 6 AND 7

The pitches we have used thus far are the notes of the diatonic scale plus chromatic embellishments a semitone away from 5 and 3. To complete the set of pitches by including all the pitches of the chromatic scale, we can add embellishments to the sixth, seventh, and first degrees of the diatonic scale. It is imperative to keep the tonality frame of the melody to be read firmly in mind when learning these chromatic tones. Otherwise you will have no sense of the true tonal function of these chromatic pitches, and you may even lose your fundamental sense of tonality.

In melodies based on the pitches of the major scale, the sixth scale degree can be embellished by pitches a semitone above and below it, as in the second and sixth measures of the melody below.

Example 3

Both of these patterns can be read with ease if you conceive of the chromatically altered pitches *in relation to the sixth scale degree:* the first as a *lower* inflection of 6, the second as an *upper* inflection of 6.[1]

---

[1] These chromatic inflections of diatonic pitches are sometimes called *secondary leading tones,* since their effect is similar to the leading tone-tonic relation in a scale.

Sing the following patterns to gain familiarity with the chromatic embellishments of 6 in major keys. Sing them in every key, using *sol-fa* syllables or scale-degree numbers for every pitch except the chromatic, as the example indicates. After you know the basic pattern well, use note names.

Example 4

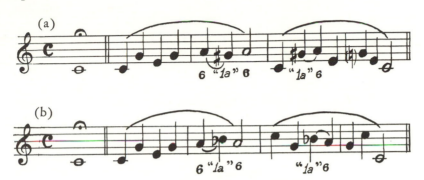

Although these chromatic pitches should be learned as embellishments of 6, they will not always occur in this simple relation in melodies. Even when they do not, however, it will be easier to sing them accurately if you think of them in relation to 6. (After considerable experience in music reading, you will be able to think of them as distinct pitches in their own right.) In the melody below, the pitch skip from *E* to *B♭* is easier to sing if you think of the *B♭* as a semitone above 6, even though 6 does not appear until the sixth measure.

Example 5

We can regard the flatted seventh degree as the lower embellishment of 7, as well as the upper embellishment of 6. The notation of this chromatic pitch would influence your decision to relate it to one or the other, as we discussed earlier (p. 171) in regard to inflections of 5 and 3. In pattern (a) below, the notation indicates 6 as the easier pitch of orientation, while pattern (b) indicates 7.

Example 6

Because the pitch of the seventh degree itself is difficult to imagine in some patterns, it does not always provide a useful reference point. For example, since the passage below hovers around the lower degrees of the scale, 6 is a better reference for the chromatic *Ab*.

Example 7

But in the next pattern, which uses the upper scale degrees (6, 7, 1) 7 is a more suitable reference pitch for the same *Ab*.

Example 8

When you scan a melody before singing it, you should note the occurrence of chromatic embellishing tones and decide which pitch is a more suitable reference.

Learn the following pattern in the key of *C* major, using numbers or *sol-fa* syllables for all notes except the indicated chromatic pitch. Then practice it in various keys, using note names.

Example 9

## CHROMATIC EMBELLISHMENT OF 1 OR 2

The only remaining chromatic pitch is the one that forms an upper leading-tone relation with 1 and a lower leading-tone relation with 2. As with the previous chromatic relations, the notation and context will determine the diatonic pitch to which the chromatic pitch is best related. The example in *C* major, below, illustrates two occurrences of the same pitch.

Example 10

In the first instance, the chromatic pitch is related to 1; in the second instance, it is related to 2.

Practice each of the following patterns carefully until you can sing it easily and accurately without referring to the example or to the piano. Then sing it in different keys, using note names rather than scale-degree names.

## PRACTICE PATTERNS

(a) major

(b) minor

(c) minor

## PRACTICE MELODIES

(a)

(b)

(j)

# MELODIES FROM LITERATURE

1. Binchois

2. Morales

3. U.S.

4. U.S.

5. U.S.

6. Handel

7. Haydn

8. Verdi

9. Brahms

10. Byrd

11. Lully

12. Bach

13. Haydn

14. Schubert

15. Beethoven

16. Grieg

17. Handel

18. Beethoven

19. Purcell

20. Telemann

21. Rameau

22. Handel

23. Mozart[2]

[2] Divisions of the basic duration as well as the basic duration itself can be divided into triplets. Such triplets should present no special difficulties.

24. Chopin

25. Chopin

26. Mozart

27. Schubert

28. Schubert

29. Schumann

30. Donizetti

31. Spain

32. Mozart

33. Sweden

34. Mozart

35. Mozart

36. Beethoven

37. Mozart

38. Schubert

39. Mozart

40. Schubert

41. Schubert

42. Beethoven

43. Offenbach

# 12

---

# *THE MODES; INTERBEAT SYNCOPATION*

---

## *DORIAN, PHRYGIAN, LYDIAN, AND MIXOLYDIAN MODES*

Although most music of the Western world uses major and minor scales as pitch bases, there is also a sizable body of music that uses pitch bases that deviate slightly from these scales. Any seven-pitch scale that does not follow the intervallic structure of the major or the minor scales is called a *mode*. Music based on such a scale is *modal* music.

Two of the scales we have discussed have modal names. The major scale is called the *Ionian mode;* the natural minor scale is the *Aeolian mode.*[1] (The mode names are derived from the names of ancient Greek tribes.) You will remember that the characteristic features of the latter scale are a minor mediant and a seventh degree a whole step below tonic.

Example 1      Aeolian mode (natural minor)

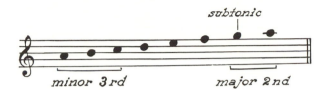

But the remaining modes have no counterparts in the major or minor scales. The diagram that follows illustrates them and shows the distinguishing intervals of each. They are written with different tonics so that no accidentals are needed;[2] when transposed to other pitch levels, they require note alterations just as major or minor scales do.

Example 2

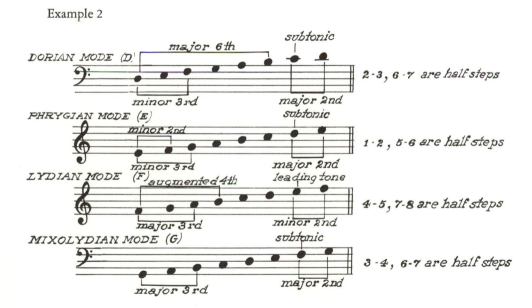

---

[1] In a strict sense, *scale* and *mode* are synonyms; however, traditional usage has imposed upon current thought a distinction between scales and modes.

[2] Still another mode, called *Locrian,* was postulated by some medieval musicians just to fill out the system by beginning a scale on the remaining pitch, *B.* This mode is not used in enough melodies to justify our attention, however. On a tonic of *B* it consists of the series B–C–D–E–F–G–A–B.

(Note that each of these modes can be played on the piano using only successive white keys if the tonics shown above—*D* for Dorian, *E* for Phrygian, *F* for Lydian, *G* for Mixolydian—are used.)

It is important to remember that each mode has its own unique sound and structure. Avoid thinking of any mode as part of a major or minor scale, just because the latter is more familiar. Example 3 illustrates this mistaken procedure.

Example 3

Similarly, the Dorian mode could be falsely regarded as a fragment of a major scale beginning on its second degree, the Mixolydian as a fragment of a major scale beginning on its fifth degree, and so forth.

Learn each of the following patterns as it is written here, then transpose it to other tonics and sing it using note names rather than *sol-fa* syllables or scale-degree numbers. You should also use the appropriate practice pattern as an exercise before singing any melody in the same mode.

*PRACTICE PATTERNS*

As a further exercise, the class should sing scales and modes on tonics given by the instructor.

Note that the key signatures in modal tunes serve the same purpose as in major and minor tunes; they indicate the altered notes. The notation of modal melodies is sometimes at variance with this practice, however; the accidentals that establish the mode of the melody are sometimes added within its course. The "Practice Melodies" at the end of this chapter are notated in both ways: some use key signatures that are appropriate to the mode, others use signatures that require accidentals in the melody. Later we shall encounter melodies which mix two or more modes, using different modes in different passages.

## INTERBEAT SYNCOPATION

In Chapter 1, we noted that rhythmic accent is a basic property of melody; meter is nothing more than the periodic grouping of a series of accented and unaccented pulses.

Once a particular pattern of grouping has been established in a melody, any deviation from it tends to disrupt rhythmic flow. When the deviation is a displaced accent, it creates what is called *syncopation*.

There are several ways in which an accent can be displaced. One way is through an irregular agogic accent.[3] When the tones of a pattern are of different lengths, we tend to hear the longer tones as more prominent or accented. Given the series of articulations in Ex. 4 (a), we would probably hear the whole pattern as in (b) rather than (c), because in (b) the longer tones occur at regular intervals.

Example 4

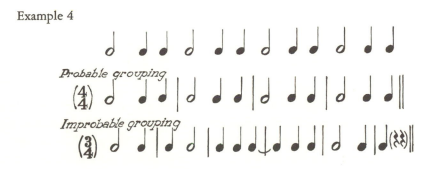

Since a longer tone draws attention to itself, it can momentarily disrupt the regular flow of a meter when it occurs on a beat that is ordinarily not accented.

Example 5

In this passage, the bracketed measures are syncopated because the agogic accent falls on a pulse that is normally weak.

---

[3] See Chapter 1, p. 3, for a discussion of agogic accent.

An even more disruptive syncopation results when there is a rest on the first beat of a measure. The rhythm in Ex. 5 can be changed to illustrate this greater displacement of the normal accent.

Example 6

This is still rhythmic displacement by an agogic accent.

Syncopation also results when a *dynamic* accent is placed on a pulse that is normally weak. In a triple meter, for instance, the metric accent falls on the first pulse; if a dynamic accent occurs on any other pulse, syncopation results.

Example 7

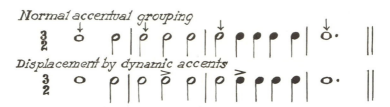

A still greater degree of syncopation results when both agogic and dynamic accents fall on a weak beat.

Example 8

There is another, more subtle, kind of syncopation. In their striving to create melodies of extreme smoothness, early renaissance composers coined the expression "high note law" to describe this displacement of the regular accent. The principle is simple: a pitch that is approached by a leap from a lower pitch is slightly more important. If this higher pitch occurs on a normally weak pulse, a discernible displacement of the metric grouping results. The fifth and sixth measures of Ex. 9 contain this sort of syncopation; the renotation shows the disruption more clearly.

Example 9

### SUPERTRIPLETS

　　　　The second form of metric disruption that we shall discuss in this chapter is slightly more drastic; one basic metric frame is briefly imposed upon another. We have already dealt with this kind of deviation in the discussion of triplets in simple meters. The same deviation can occur in durations greater than the basic duration, as a *supertriplet*.

Example 10

　　　　The supertriplet is sometimes difficult to perform accurately, because it demands the ability to conceive of a three-part pattern imposed upon a two-part framework.

　　　　The regular triplet offers a handy framework for learning to perform supertriplets. As the example below shows, a syncopated grouping of two regular triplets is the exact parallel of a supertriplet in $\frac{2}{4}$ or $\frac{4}{4}$.

Example 11

The same principle can be applied, of course, to $\frac{2}{2}$ or $\frac{2}{8}$.

　　　　The following exercises can be useful in learning supertriplets. Attempt the second pattern only when you can perform the first with ease.

### PRACTICE PATTERNS

*DUPLETS*

In compound meters the parallel of the triplet is the duplet, the imposition of a two-part division on the usual three-part background. This irregular pattern usually proves to be less of an obstacle for readers than the supertriplet.

Example 12

Use the pattern below to practice duplets in a compound meter.

Example 13

Another (equally correct) notation of the duplet uses the proper dotted-note values to create the two-part division. Example 13 is renotated in this way in Ex. 14. Contemporary musicians generally prefer to use the duplet sign, however.

Example 14

# MELODIES FROM LITERATURE

1. Greece

2. Traditional

3. Medieval

4. Hofhaimer

5. U.S.

6. U.S.

7. U.S.

8. U.S.

9. U.S.

10. Flotow

11. Massenet

12. U.S.

13. U.S.

14. Hungary (Bartók)

15. Hungary (Bartók)

16. Liszt[4]

17. Hungary (Kodály)

18. U.S.

---

[4] In compound meters, a *quadruplet* (measure 8) equals two duplets.

19. Schumann

20. Borodin

21. von Reuenthal

22. U.S.

23. Mozart

24. Beethoven

25. Mozart

# 13

## MODULATION AND MUTATION IN MELODY

Most of the melodies that people sing in public gatherings or whistle or hum in their moments of leisure are organized around a single tonic and use a limited set of pitches—a single scale. Many melodies are slightly more complex, however; they may change tonics, exchange one kind of scale for another, or do both.

The shift from one tonic to another is called

*modulation.* Notice in the melody below that the first two measures are clearly organized around *C,* whereas the second two measures repeat the same melodic contour in *G,* a perfect fourth lower. This is a simple and brief example of a modulation.

Example 1        Russia

The next example is a more typical modulation, because of the location of the contrasting passage; the outer passages are in the key of *A* major, while the brief middle passage shifts to *F♯* minor.

Example 2        Chopin

You could, of course, think of every pitch in this melody as related to the pitches of the *A* major scale. This strains the imagination unnecessarily, however, for the *C♯-F♯* motion at the ends of measures 9 and 11 (a movement from a weak to a strong metric accent) and the *E♯* that precedes this motion force us to adopt a new tonality frame, *C♯-F♯-A.* Read through Ex. 2 slowly. Just before measure 9, stop and sing 3, 6, and 1 of the preceding scale as a new tonality frame. At the fermata in measure 13, relate the *C♯* to the old tonic, *A,* and continue in *A* major. This procedure is shown below.

Example 3

To accurately and fluently read any melody in which a modulation occurs, you must learn to orient yourself to the new tonality frame. In most cases a pitch in the old key can be used as a pitch reference for the new key. In the Chopin melody, *A,* which is tonic in measure 8, changes to the mediant in the tonality frame of measures 9–13, and *C♯*, which is the dominant in measure 13, changes to the mediant in the tonality frame of the final section.

The modulations in the melodies in this chapter are relatively easy to sing, for they use keys that have many pitches in common. (In the Chopin example, *A* major and *F♯* minor have all the same pitches except the *E♯* seventh degree in the minor section.) When two keys have at least six pitches in common, they are called *near-related keys.* Every major and minor key has five near-related keys; the diagram below shows the near-related keys of *C* major. Notice that only the natural minor scales are used, and each pitch not in the *C* major scale is circled in the related scales.

Example 4

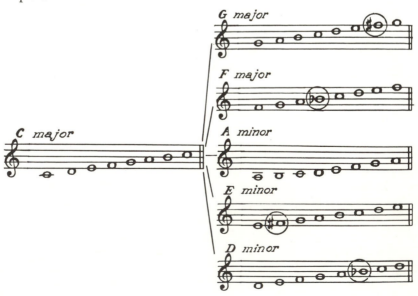

In another kind of tonal change, called *mutation,* the scale is changed but the tonic is not. In the melody below, the first section is organized around *F* and uses the natural minor scale. But in measure 9, the melody suddenly changes to the parallel major scale—*F* major.

Example 5        Sweden

When reading a melody in which a modulation occurs, you should find the tonality frame of the new key and its relation to the old, and note any pitches where the shift occurs that can serve as points of reference for both keys. Until you become relatively fluent, you should also sing through the tonality frames for both sections involved in the modulation *before* you sing the melody.

The patterns which follow are rhythmically simple, so that full attention can be directed to the pitch problems involved. Each pattern incorporates a kind of modulation or mutation that will occur in the melodies from literature at the end of this chapter. Study each carefully before you sing it. Determine the relation between the two keys, the necessary pitch reorientation, and the place where the key change occurs. If you use a piano, use it only to establish the tonality frames before you sing and to check the final pitch afterward. *Never play the melody before you read it.*

*PRACTICE PATTERNS*

---

[1] To be read: "2 becomes 5."

# MELODIES FROM LITERATURE

1. Adam de la Halle

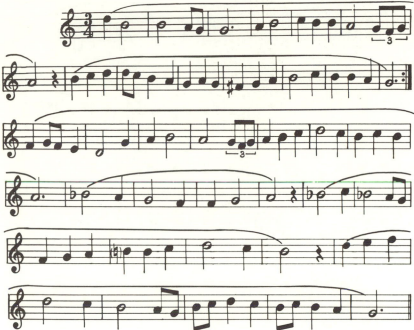

2. Machaut

3. Dunstable

4. U.S.

5. Zumsteeg

6. Schumann

7. U.S.

8. Purcell

9. Beethoven

10. Offenbach

11.  Pergolesi

12.  Bach

13.  U.S.

14.  Haydn

15. Mascagni

16. Pergolesi

17. Schiedt

18. Hungary (Kodály)

19. Hungary (Kodály)

20. German chorale (Bach)

21. Offenbach

22. Diabelli

23. Brahms

24. Handel

25. Donizetti

26. Purcell

27. Schubert

28. Schröter

### 29. Monteverdi

### 30. Bach

### 31. Telemann

# 14

## *CHANGING AND COMPOSITE METERS*

*CHANGING METERS*

       Occasionally the meter of a melody will change between sections, or even within a single section. This is sometimes called *mixed meters* or *successive polymeter*. In many instances the change of meter presents no real difficulties, because the basic duration does not change. For example, the quarter note is the basic duration of both

233

meters in the melody below; only the number of basic durations per measure changes.

Example 1     U.S.

When simple and compound meters are combined in a melody, the situation is more complicated. For precision, the composer should specify the relation between the basic durations of the two meters. When he does not, the performer must decide what the composer intended, and this is not always easy. When no direction is given, you can assume that any note value in the second meter has the same duration that it had in the first meter. In the passage below, for example, you can assume that the quarter note has the same duration in every measure.

Example 2     Weelkes

To avoid confusion, most contemporary composers mark their music to show the precise relation between two successive meters. In the following example, ♪ = ♪ means that an eighth note in the first meter equals an eighth note in the second meter.

Example 3

In some older music, however, the meaning of this sign is reversed, and the first note refers to the second meter, as in Ex. 4.

Example 4

To avoid misinterpretation, many contemporary composers add arrows which show unequivocally the meter to which each note value applies: ←♪ = ♩→ .

When reading melodies that use mixed meters, you should try, when it is possible, to establish continuity by keeping in mind a constant duration for a note value that occurs in both meters. For example, in the melody below the eighth note should be used in this way.

Example 5

The practice melodies that follow have relatively simple pitch patterns. Since the melodies from literature at the end of the chapter are not limited in this respect, you should practice them only after you can read the practice melodies fluently.

*PRACTICE MELODIES*

## COMPOSITE METERS

In all simple and compound meters the measures are evenly divisible by 2 or by 3. In *composite*[2] meters this is not possible, for, unlike simple and compound meters, they consist of unequal basic durations.

---

[1] When the absence of metric regularity makes constant signature changes more confusing than helpful, a few composers have discarded meter signatures.

[2] Sometimes called *complex* or *asymmetrical* meters.

The easiest composite meter to learn is probably $\frac{5}{8}$ (or $\frac{5}{16}$ or $\frac{5}{4}$). As a beginning, practice the following pattern; each note is of equal duration and the first note of every measure is stressed. It is essential at this point to feel each measure as a grouping of five equal units.

Example 6

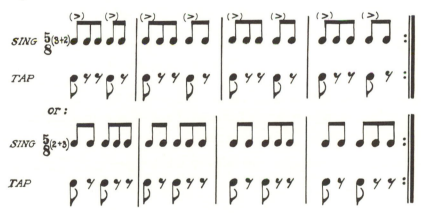

The equal units of any composite meter (represented by eighth notes in Ex. 6) are usually regarded as divisions of *unequal* basic durations. For example, the eighth notes of the passage above would normally be grouped with accents on notes (1) and (4), establishing a 3 + 2 grouping, or on notes (1) and (3), establishing a 2 + 3 grouping. Example 7 shows both of these scansions.

Example 7

The reader must determine the grouping that predominates in the melody he is reading. In many melodies the same grouping occurs constantly; in others, one grouping merely predominates.

The grouping in Ex. 8(a) is 2 + 3; in Ex. 8(b) it is 3 + 2.

Example 8

    (a) *Billy the Kid* by Aaron Copland. Piano solo arrangement by Lucas Foss.

(b) Spain

Sing the two melodies above in two ways: first while tapping five rapid pulses corresponding to the five equal eighth notes per measure; then while tapping only the basic duration pattern of each measure. For melody (a) this is a *short-long* pattern ( ♩ ♩. ), while for (b) it is a *long-short* pattern ( ♩. ♩ ).

At first, we shall deal with melodies whose rhythms are grouped in patterns of only one kind: 2 + 3, 3 + 2, and so forth. These unequal basic durations can be expressed with a tap (as in the second performances of the melodies in Ex. 8) or a conducting pattern.

For composite meters performed at tempos that are not extremely slow, use a conducting pattern that alternates slow and fast motions corresponding to the long and short values of the basic durations. The two-beat pattern learned earlier for duple meters is used for both the rhythms below. The speed of each stroke of the arm is adjusted, however, to fit the length of the basic durations.

Example 9     Conducting patterns for quintuple meters ($\frac{5}{8}, \frac{5}{4}, \frac{5}{16}$)

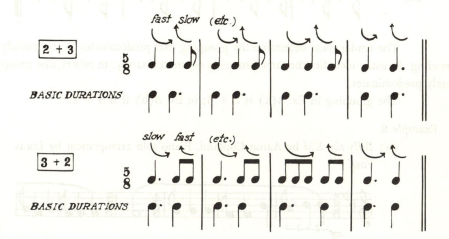

In any event, you must make certain that each note value is accorded its rightful duration. One common (and comical!) error in reading complex meters results from making all basic durations equal. For example, the Copland melody, Ex. 8(a), might be misread as $\frac{2}{4}$ meter.

Example 10      Misreading of Copland melody as $\frac{2}{4}$

A correct reading demands *unequal* basic durations, as below.

Example 11      Correct version of Copland melody

Many melodies in complex meters do not have a regular pattern of twos and threes; they may change from a 2–3 grouping to the opposite 3–2 so frequently that no pattern is established as a norm. In such melodies, the reader must regard each eighth note (in $\frac{5}{8}$, $\frac{7}{8}$, and $\frac{8}{8}$) or each quarter note (in $\frac{5}{4}$ and $\frac{7}{4}$) as a basic duration. In this text, the groupings in each melody in a complex meter will be readily distinguishable; when a variation of the grouping occurs, it can be regarded as a "syncopation."

Before reading the practice melody section, perform the practice patterns below. For each phrase use a tap or a conducting pattern as follows:

1. For $\frac{5}{8}$ and $\frac{5}{4}$ meter, use a two-beat tap or conducting pattern, long-short or short-long depending upon the grouping that dominates the melody.

2. For $\frac{7}{8}$ and $\frac{7}{4}$ meter, use a three-beat tap or conducting pattern, long-short-short or short-short-long depending upon the grouping that dominates the melody.

3. For $\frac{8}{8}$ meter (3 + 3 + 2, 3 + 2 + 3, or 2 + 3 + 3) use a three-beat tap or conducting pattern, long-long-short, long-short-long, or short-long-long depending upon the grouping that dominates the melody.

PRACTICE PATTERNS

PRACTICE MELODIES

(e)

(f)

(g)

# MELODIES FROM LITERATURE

### 1. Moussorgsky

### 2. Russia (Rimsky-Korsakov)

### 3. Hungary (Kodály)

### 4. Falla

5. Dufay

6. France

7. Hungary (Bartók)

8. Hungary (Kodály)

9. U.S.

10. U.S.

11. U.S.

12. U.S.

13. U.S.

14. U.S.

15. U.S.

16. Rumania

17. Morgan

18. Hungary (Bartók)

19. Brahms

20. Spain

21. Morley

22. Weelkes

23. U.S.

24. Gounod

25. Hungary (Bartók)

26. Mexico

27. Hungary (Kodály)

28. Falla

29. U.S.

30. Tchaikovsky

# APPENDIX

# Glossary of Musical Signs

 STACCATO—Dots above or below notes indicate shorter durations. For example, (a) should be performed as in (b).

(a)

(b)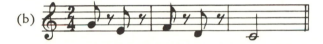

 TENUTO—Opposite of *staccato*; note is held for complete duration, undiminished in loudness.

 STRESS or ACCENT—Unusual stress at beginning of tone.

FERMATA or HOLD—Duration of the note or rest is prolonged.

 CRESCENDO—Increasing loudness.

 DECRESCENDO or DIMINUENDO—Decreasing loudness.

DOUBLE SHARP—Note is raised two semitones.

**bb**

DOUBLE FLAT—Note is lowered two semitones.

REPEAT SIGN—The passage enclosed is repeated. If only the second sign appears, repeat from the beginning.

MEASURE REPEAT—The previous measure is repeated. The following sign indicates that two measures are repeated:

Repeat from the sign (*Segno*).

D.S.
*Dal Segno*

FIRST AND SECOND ENDINGS—Repeat, omitting the measure or measures of the first ending the second time. Thus (a) below is performed as in (b).

(a)

(b)

# *Glossary of Foreign Terms*

(All terms are Italian except where noted.)

ACCELERANDO—Growing faster.

ADAGIO—Slow.

AFFETTUOSO—Affectionately, with warmth.

ALLA—In the style of.

ALLEGRETTO—Moderately fast (slower than *allegro*).

ALLEGRO—Fast, cheerful.

ANDANTE—Moderately slow (walking tempo).

ANDANTINO—Slightly quicker than *andante*.

ANIMATO—Animated.

ANIMÉ(Fr.)—Animated.

ASSAI—Very. (ALLEGRO ASSAI—Very fast.)

A TEMPO—Resume original tempo.

BEN—Well, very.

BRIO—Spirit, vigor.

CANTABILE—In a smooth, singing style.

COMODO—At a leisurely speed.

CON—With.

CRESCENDO (*Cresc.*)—Growing louder.

DA CAPO (*D.C.*)—from the beginning (from the "cap" or "top").

DAL SEGNO (*D.S.*)—From the sign ( 𝄋 ), frequently near the beginning.

DECIDÉ(Fr.)—Decided, definite.

DECISO—Decisively, boldly.

DECRESCENDO (*Decr., Decresc.*)—Decreasing in loudness.

DIMINUENDO (*Dim., Dimin.*)—Decreasing in loudness.

DI MOLTO—Very, extremely.

DOLCE—Sweetly, tenderly.

DOLENTE—Doleful.

E—And.

EINFACH (Ger.)—Simply.

ESPRESSIVO—Expressively (implies heightened emotion).

ET (Fr.)—And.

FINE—End.

FORTE (*f*)—Loud, strong.

FORTISSIMO (*ff*)—Very loud, very strong.

FRISCH (Ger.)—Brisk, lively.

FRÖHLICH (Ger.)—Joyful.

FUOCO, CON—With fire.

GAI (Fr.)—Gay.

GIOCOSO—Playful.

GIUSTO—Strict, exact.

GRACIEUX (Fr.)—Graceful.

GRAVE—Solemn, very slow.

GRAZIOSO—Graceful.

INNIG (Ger.)—Heartfelt.

LANGSAM (Ger.)—Slow.

LARGHETTO—Slow, but not as slow as *largo*.

LARGO—Slow, broad.

LEBHAFT (Ger.)—Lively, animated.

LÉGER (Fr.)—Light, delicate.

LEGGIERO, LEGGERO—Light, delicate.

LEISE (Ger.)—Soft.

LENT (Fr.)—Slow.

LENTO—Slow, but faster than *adagio* or *largo*.

LIEBLICH (Ger.)—Charming, sweet.

MA—But.

MÄCHTIG (Ger.)—Mighty, powerful.

MÄSSIG (Ger.)—Moderate.

MAESTOSO—Majestic, with dignity.

MARCATO—Marked, with emphasis.

MENO—Less.

MENUETTO—Minuet.

MESTO—Sad, mournful.

MEZZO FORTE (*mf*)—Moderately loud.

MEZZO PIANO (*mp*)—Moderately soft.

MODERATO—Moderate.

MODÉRÉ (Fr.)—Moderate.

MOLTO—Very.

MOSSO—Motion. (MENO MOSSO—Less motion, slower.)

MOTO, CON—With motion.

PARLANDO—Speaking.

PESANTE—Heavy.

PIANISSIMO (*pp*)—Very soft, very quiet.

PIANO (*p*)—Soft, quiet.

POCO—Little. (POCO A POCO—Little by little, gradually.)

PRESTO—Very fast.

QUASI—As if, like, similar to.

RALLENTANDO—Growing slower.

RISOLUTO—Resolute.

RITARDANDO (*rit., ritard.*)—Growing slower.

SCHERZANDO—Joking, playful.

SCHNELL (Ger.)—Fast.

SCHWER (Ger.)—Heavy.

SEMPLICE—Simple.

SICILIANO—A type of pastoral dance.

SIMILE—Similarly, in the same manner.

SOSTENUTO—Sustained.

SPIRITO—Spirit.

SUBITO—Suddenly.

SOSPIRANDO—Sighing, plaintive.

TANTO—Much, as much. (NON TANTO—Not too much.)

TENERAMENTE—Tenderly.

TENUTO—Sustained.

TRANQUILLO—Tranquil, quiet.

TRÈS (Fr.)—Very.

TROPPO—Too, too much.
(MA NON TROPPO—But not too much.)

VIF (Fr.)—Lively, fast.

VIGOROSO—Vigorous.

VIVACE—Lively, quick.

VIVO—Fast, animated.

ZART (Ger.)—Tender, soft.

ZIEMLICH (Ger.)—Moderately, rather.

# Index